Transport Statistics Report

GW00372449

Vehicle Licensing Statistics 1993

Motor vehicles currently licensed, new registrations, goods vehicle statistics.

Published October 1994

London: HMSO

Brief extracts from this publication may be reproduced provided the source is fully acknowledged. Proposals for the reproduction of larger extracts should be addressed to the Copyright Section, Her Majesty's Stationery Office, St Crispins, Duke Street, Norwich, NR3 1PD.

Governmental Statistical Service

A service of statistical information and advice is provided to the Government by specialist staffs employed in individual Departments. Statistics are made generally available through their publications and further information and advice on them can be obtained from the Departments concerned

Enquiries about the contents of this publication should be made to:

Department of Transport
STA2 Division
Room A615
Romney House
43 Marsham Street
London SW1P 3PY
Telephone: 0171 276 8559

The Department of Transport is often prepared to sell unpublished data. Further information can be obtained from the above address.

Produced from camera ready copy supplied by the Department.

The price of this publication has been set to contribute to the preparations costs incurred at the Department of Transport.

CONTENTS   PAGE

Introduction: 1

Commentary and charts: 2

Notes and definitions: 12

Tables:

Motor vehicles currently licensed

    1 By taxation group: 1983-1993.   21

    2 By taxation group: vehicle details: 1983-1993.   22

    3 By body type: 1983-1993.   24

    4 By year of 1st registration: 1993.   25

    5 By propulsion type: 1993.   27

    6 Motorcars currently licensed: Age distribution of stock and   27
    survival rates: 1987, 1990 & 1993.

    7 Motorcars currently licensed: By year of 1st registration and   28
    engine size: 1993.

    8 By taxation group, county and region. 1993.   29

Motor vehicles currently licensed - historic series

    9 By taxation group: 1903-1982.   31

Motor vehicles registered for the first time

    10 By taxation group: 1983-1993.   32

    11 By taxation group: vehicle details: 1983-1993.   33

    12 By county, with related information. 1993.   35

    13 Seasonally adjusted series: by month: 1987-1993.   37

Motor vehicles registered for the first time - historic series

14 By taxation group: 1951-1982   38

International comparisons of vehicle stock

15 Passenger vehicle stock: 1981 & 1991   39

16 Passenger vehicles per head: 1981 & 1991   39

17 Road goods vehicles: 1981 & 1991   40

Goods vehicles statistics

18 Goods vehicle stock at end of year: 1982-1993.   41

19 Goods vehicle stock: by gross weight and axle configuration: 1993.   41

20 Goods vehicle stock: by taxation group and axle configuration: 1993.   42

21 Goods vehicle stock: by gross vehicle weight and type of body: 1993.   43

22 Goods vehicle stock: by gross vehicle weight and year of 1st registration: 1993.   44

23 Goods vehicle stock: by year of 1st registration and type of body: 1993.   45

24 Goods vehicle stock: by county, region and axle configuration: 1993.   46

25 Goods vehicle stock at end of year: by year of 1st registration: 1983-1993.   48

26 Goods vehicle stock at end of year: by gross vehicle weight: 1984-1993.   49

27 Goods vehicle stock at end of year: by gross vehicle weight, axle configuration: 1988-1993   50

VEHICLE LICENSING STATISTICS 1993

Motor vehicles currently licensed, new registrations, goods vehicle statistics.

Introduction

This edition of 'Vehicle Licensing Statistics: Great Britain: 1993' continues to pursue the aim set out in the 1992 edition of combining in a single volume information previously published in various other reports. The major addition to this report is the inclusion of statistics previously given in 'Goods Vehicles in Great Britain'.

The tables taken from that source have been reset to occupy less page space and keep the cost of the publication down. Despite the inclusion of additional commentary, charts and tables, this volume contains 50 pages compared with a combined total of 58 for the two original reports. The extra contents have prompted the addition of a sub-title to describe the major components of the report.

At the same time, all tables concerned with currently licensed stock in this volume are now drawn from a single source, the Directorate of Statistics Vehicle Information Database (VID). This database holds vehicle records supplied by the Driver and Vehicle Licensing Agency (DVLA) at quarterly intervals. This eliminates inconsistencies which used to arise between information drawn from the 'annual vehicles census' analyses, the 'goods vehicle census' analyses, and the 'goods vehicle list' in previous published statistics.

Although the basic data on the database are the same as those held by DVLA, derived statistics differ slightly from those produced by DVLA because the opportunity has been taken to update and revise certain definitions embodied in the computer programmes in use for many years at DVLA.

Finally, this report contains some new tables and some expanded tables, mainly to provide extra regional statistics including county information. Cross reference information on tables is given below in the notes on goods vehicles statistics (section 5) to assist readers who may wish to compare results in this report with those from the 1992 edition of 'Goods Vehicles in Great Britain' and earlier publications. Further details of all these developments are given in the notes and definitions section below.

Commentary and charts

Licensed vehicle stock 1983-1993

-     The total vehicle stock in Great Britain at the end of 1993 was estimated to be 24.83 million vehicles, of which 20.75 million vehicles, or about 84%, were motorcars. The next most numerous vehicle group by body type was light goods vehicles with a stock of over 1.94 million vehicles, or 8% of the total.

-     The remainder of the stock is made up of 740,000 motorcycles; 590,000 other goods vehicles; 290,000 agricultural tractors; 150,000 buses and coaches; 40,000 three wheelers; 30,000 custom built taxis; and 280,000 other assorted vehicle types. Note that a vehicle's body type is not always a reliable guide to its taxation class.

-     The final group of 280,000 other assorted vehicle types includes emergency service vehicles such as fire engines and ambulances, road repair vehicles such as road surfacers, road surface strippers, bulldozers, tar sprayers, road rollers and line painters, road maintenance vehicles such as street cleansing, snow ploughs and gritting lorries and various types of construction vehicles, cranes, shovels, diggers and excavators.

-     The total stock of vehicles has grown by an estimated 24% between the end of 1983 and the end of 1993; a rate equivalent to 2.2% per annum. Growth has been lower in recent years. Since the end of 1989, the estimated total growth in vehicle stock is 3.7%; a rate equivalent to 0.9% per annum.

-     Growth in motorcar stock totalled 32.0% between 1983 and 1993, equivalent to 2.8% per annum.

-     The stock of vehicles with goods body types remained relatively constant between 1983 and 1987, grew by about 5.5% between the end of 1988 and the end of 1989, and has since declined. The stock at the end of 1993 was 587,000 vehicles, an estimated overall reduction of 6.7% since 1983, and a reduction of 11.9% since 1988.

-     Motorcycle stocks have declined steadily over the last ten years, by an estimated 48.6% in total, a rate equivalent to 6.4% fewer vehicles per year. The overall reduction of roughly 600,000 motorcycles helps explain why total vehicle stocks have grown more slowly than motorcar stocks.

Licensed vehicle stock 1983-93: By body type

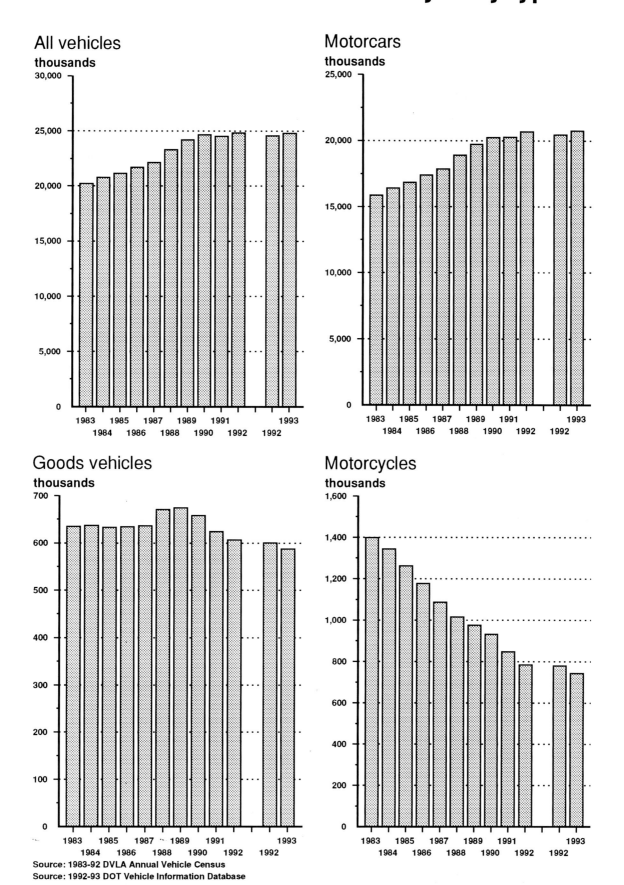

All vehicles
thousands

Motorcars
thousands

Goods vehicles
thousands

Motorcycles
thousands

Source: 1983-92 DVLA Annual Vehicle Census
Source: 1992-93 DOT Vehicle Information Database

Vehicles registered for the first time 1983 to 1993

- In a typical year somewhere between 2.0 and 2.5 million new vehicles are registered at the Driver and Vehicle Licensing Agency. In the past ten years, most vehicles were registered in 1988 and 1989 with 2.72 and 2.83 million vehicles and least in 1991 and 1992 when 1.92 and 1.90 million vehicles were registered respectively. Registrations in 1993, at 2.07 million, were 9% higher than the 1992 figure but remain 10% below the 1983 total of 2.31 million. Most new registrations are not additions to current stocks but replacements for existing stock.

- Registrations of new motorcars followed a similar pattern, with peaks in 1988 and 1989 and a trough in 1991 and 1992. Registrations in 1993, at 1.78 million, were 1.5% lower than in 1983. Between 1983 and 1993 the proportion of new vehicles registered to a keeper with a company title has increased from 39% to 52%, while the residue, registered to private keepers has reduced by the corresponding amount.

- New vehicles registered in goods vehicle taxation classes also reached their highest levels in 1988 and 1989 with 63 and 65 thousand new registrations respectively, and low points in 1991 and 1992 with 29 thousand new registrations in each of those two years. The relative gap between these high and low points was much greater than for other vehicle types. Registrations in 1993 at 33 thousand vehicles were 14% higher than in 1992, but remained 30% below the 1983 figure and 49% below the 1989 peak.

- Although registrations of new motorcycles showed little change between 1987 and 1988 and even increased slightly in 1989, registrations have shown a considerable overall decline in the ten year period from 1983. The number of new motorcycles registered in 1993 at 58 thousand was 66% lower than the figure for 1983. Whilst, in part, this may reflect consumer choice, motorcycle driving tests have also become more difficult and learner motorcyclists subject to additional regulations as the government, as part of its road safety policy, has tried to reduce the number of motorcyclists killed and injured on Britain's roads.

- In 1982 two part motorcycle tests were introduced and provisional motorcycle licenses restricted to two years. In 1983 learner motorcyclists were only allowed to ride machines up to 125 cc's. In 1989 accompanied motorcycle testing became mandatory. In 1990 compulsory basic training for learner motorcyclists was introduced, and learner motorcyclists were banned from carrying pillion passengers.

Vehicles registered for the 1st time 1983-93

All vehicles
thousands

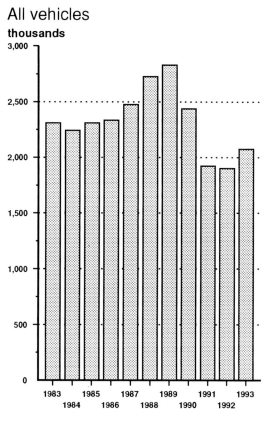

Motorcars
thousands

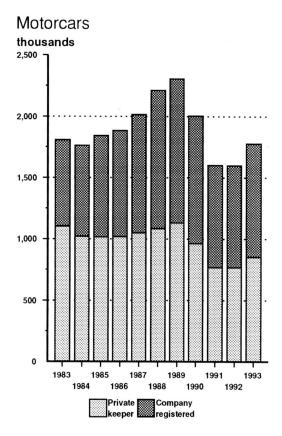

Vehicles in goods tax classes
thousands

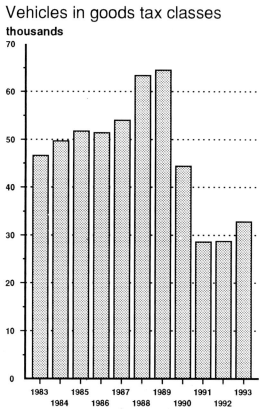

Motorcycle tax classes
thousands

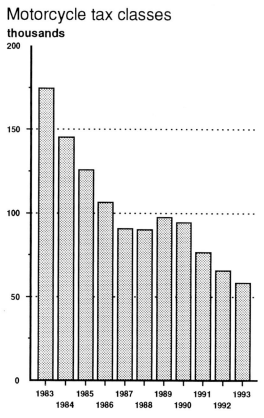

Vehicle details: 1983 and 1993 compared

-   Compared with 1983, motorcars in 1993 have a greater proportion of vehicles with engine capacities in the range 1501 to 2000 cc's, and somewhat smaller proportion with engine capacities in other groups.

-   One explanation for this may be the increased proportion of diesel powered motorcars in use, which has risen from almost none in 1983 to over 6% in 1993, and looks set to increase further, given that, by the end of 1993, diesel vehicles made up roughly 20% of new cars registered each month.

-   The taxation group for public transport vehicles, covers both taxis and buses and coaches. Compared with 1983 a smaller proportion of such vehicles fall in the group having up to four seats, that is small taxi and hackney carriages, and increased proportions into the group having from 5 to 8 seats, that is larger taxis, and the group having 9 to 32 seats, which includes minibuses and smaller buses and coaches. The proportion of larger buses and coaches, that is with 48 or more seats is little changed.

-   The greatest change in the composition of goods vehicle stock between 1983 and 1993 has been the marked increase in the proportion of vehicles in the gross weight range from 33 to 38 tonnes, as a result of changes in regulations introduced in May 1983 which increased the maximum gross vehicle weight limit from 32.5 tonnes to 38 tonnes. This, and a slight increase in the proportion of lorries in the gross weight range up to 7.5 tonnes, is mirrored by a general fall in the proportion of general goods vehicles in other weight ranges.

-   As the section on licensed stock showed, the overall stock of motorcycles has roughly halved between 1983 and 1993. Accompanying this change in numbers has been a marked upward shift in the average engine capacity of bikes in use. The proportion having engine capacities up to 50 cc's has fallen by about 15 percentage points, whereas the proportion with capacities over 500 cc's has increased from less than 10% to more than 25% of licensed stock.

Vehicle details: 1983 and 1993 compared

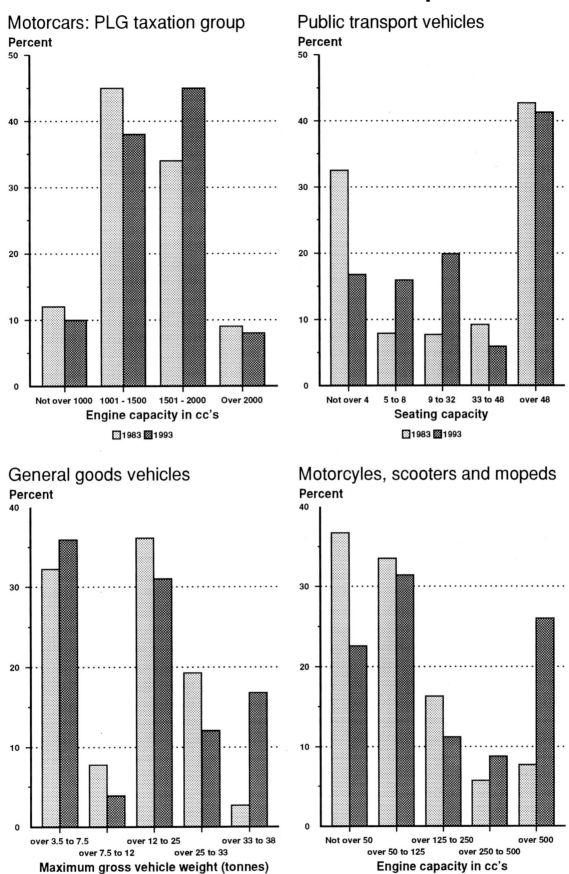

Motorcars: PLG taxation group

Percent

Engine capacity in cc's

1983 1993

Public transport vehicles

Percent

Seating capacity

1983 1993

General goods vehicles

Percent

Maximum gross vehicle weight (tonnes)

1983 1993

Motorcyles, scooters and mopeds

Percent

Engine capacity in cc's

1983 1993

Current vehicle stock: Year of first registration

-         Very few vehicles are not new when first registered. For all practical purposes therefore the year of first registration can be used to monitor the age of any sample of vehicles. For example, vehicles first registered in 1993 will, in general, be not more than one year old by the end of that year, vehicles first registered in 1992 not more than two years old at the end of 1993, etc etc.

-         The age profile of most vehicles reflects the peak in new registration which occurred in 1989. Despite wastage, the group of motorcars more than 4 years old but not more than six years old remains the largest at almost exactly 20% of licensed stock. Of currently licensed motorcars 15% are not more than two years old, but roughly four percent were registered before 1980, and are now at least 14 years old.

-         Among the common vehicle types, public transport vehicles have the largest group of old vehicles, with nearly 23% registered before 1980, and now at least 14 years old. Other age groups are roughly evenly distributed, albeit with some peaking in the 1986 to 1989 period.

-         Although motorcycles are generally among the most short lived of all vehicles, older bikes were registered in substantially greater numbers than in recent years. For example, in 1980 and 1981 a combined total of over 570,000 new bikes were registered compared with a total of 125,000 in 1992 and 1993. Despite wastage, substantial numbers of these older bikes remain in the currently licensed stock so that no two year age band up to 12 years old makes up less than 10% of current stocks.

Current vehicle stock: Year of 1st registration

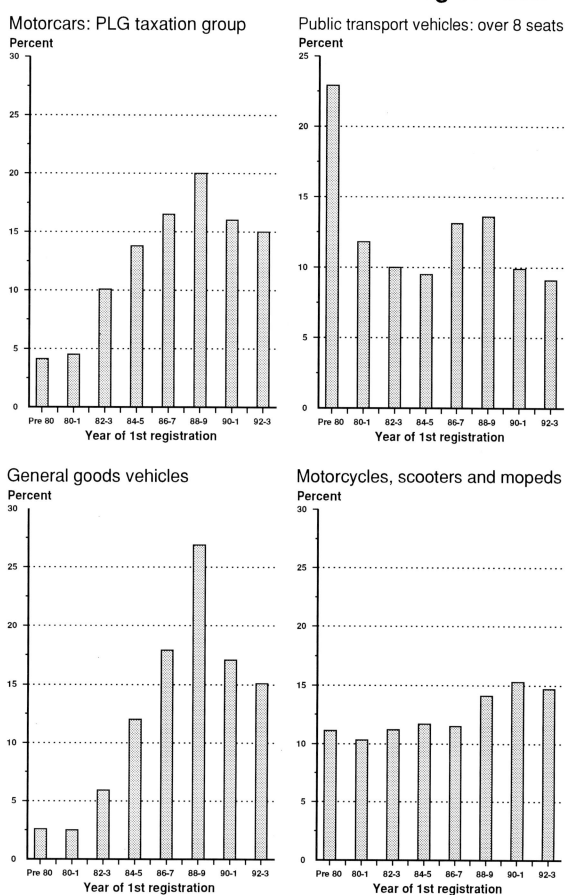

Motorcars: PLG taxation group
Percent

Public transport vehicles: over 8 seats
Percent

General goods vehicles
Percent

Motorcycles, scooters and mopeds
Percent

Goods vehicle stock 1993

-      Tables 18 onwards in this report give details of the currently licensed "goods vehicle stock". Although tabulations giving information on vehicles in goods vehicle taxation classes, and having goods vehicle construction are useful, they have some disadvantages.

-      For example, some special vehicles may be in goods vehicle taxation groups and weigh less than 3,500 kgs, which would normally result in being taxed in the Private and Light Goods group. Moreover, some heavy goods vehicles may be taxed in other groups.

-      Tables 18 onwards give statistics for a carefully defined set of currently licensed goods vehicles, all of which exceed 3,500 kgs maximum gross vehicle weight. The vehicles included are all those in taxation groups 1 to 9 (the most common heavy goods vehicle taxation groups) plus vehicles with goods vehicle body types in taxation group 26 (goods electric), taxation group 60 (crown vehicles) and taxation groups 65 to 90 (exempt vehicles).

-      The goods vehicle stock, as defined above, stood at 410,000 vehicles at the end of 1993, of which 313,000 were rigid vehicles and 98,000 articulated. This is a fall of 1% percent on 1992 and continues the decline from the 1989 peak of 478,000 vehicles.

-      Many goods vehicles are constructed to maximise the amount of goods that can be carried within regulations and taxation bands. Rigid 2 axle goods vehicles cannot exceed 17 tonnes, rigid 3 axle goods vehicles cannot exceed 24.39 tonnes and rigid 4 axle goods cannot exceed 30.49 tonnes. The maximum weight for 4 axle articulated goods vehicles is 32.5 tonnes, and for 5 axle articulated goods vehicles 38 tonnes. The maximum weight vehicle that can be driven on an ordinary driving license in 7.5 tonnes.

-      Two axle vehicles remain the most common form of rigid lorry. Two axle articulated tractor units outnumber 3 axle units by more than two to one. Most articulated tractors are licensed to pull either 3 axle trailers, or any axle trailer configuration. Articulated vehicle trailers do not need to be registered with DVLA and are not subject to vehicle excise duty. They are, however, subject to Vehicle Inspectorate roadworthiness tests, and from this source, the total stock in 1993 is estimated at roughly 225,000 trailers.

Goods vehicle stock 1993: Weight & axle details

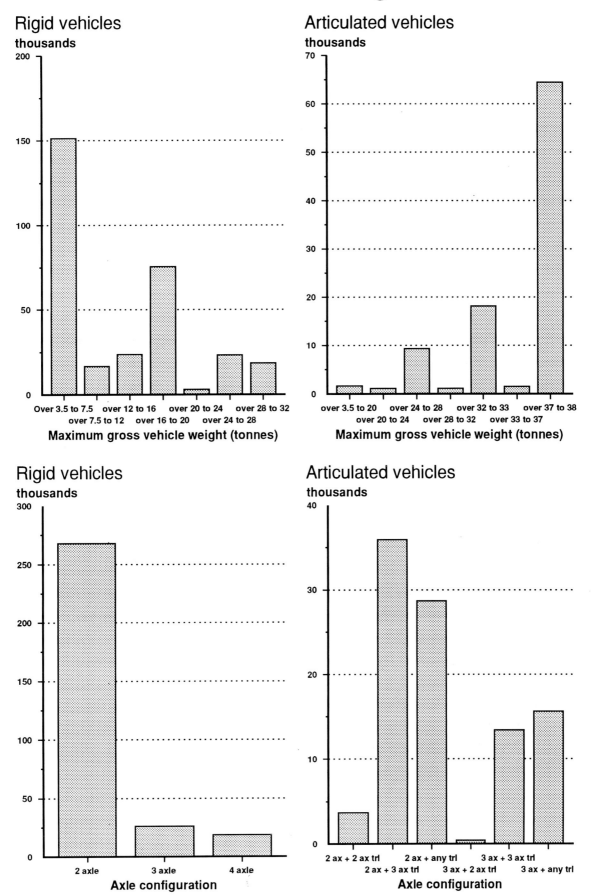

Rigid vehicles
thousands

Maximum gross vehicle weight (tonnes)

Articulated vehicles
thousands

Maximum gross vehicle weight (tonnes)

Rigid vehicles
thousands

Axle configuration

Articulated vehicles
thousands

Axle configuration

Notes and Definitions

1. NOTES ON THE VEHICLE INFORMATION DATABASE

1.1 As described in the inroduction, the Vehicle Information database (VID), is held in the Department of Transport's Statistics Directorate and updated quarterly using information suplied by DVLA. The results in this publication were produced from the VID and conform to the same standards and definitions as the earlier vehicle censuses. However, for technical reasons are considered slightly more reliable than earlier estimates.

1.2 Some vehicles have complicated licensing histories, that may include incidents such as cheques failing to clear, changes of taxation status, late payments, and one or more valid or invalid refund claims. The VID undertakes a more detailed examination of licensing history and is therefore able to provide better estimates of licensed stock on a particular date than were available from the earlier vehicle census analyses.

2. NOTES ON CURRENTLY LICENSED STOCK STATISTICS: TABLES 1 to 8

Effects of using the Vehicle Information Database

2.1 The net effect of the change to the VID as the main source of statistics on currently licensed stock was to produce a small reduction - of the order of 1% - in the estimated levels of licensed stock. Although this is a small change in absolute terms, it is relatively large compared to the annual growth in licensed stock, which, since 1983, has averaged roughly 2.3% per annum.

2.2 A number of main tables showing time series of licensed stock have therefore been broken at 1992, and show both the series based on previous census analyses up to 1992, and 1992 and 1993 results taken from the VID. Estimates of changes between years before and after 1992 can be made by combining the changes from the two series.

Census methods used in earlier publications

2.3 Censuses based entirely on the record of licensed vehicles at DVLA began on 31 December 1978, and subsequent counts have been taken on the last day of the year up to and including 31st December 1992. There are two important differences between the censuses based entirely on DVLA records and censuses prior to 1978.

2.4 Firstly, censuses derived from DVLA records were based on a single point (one day) in time. In previous censuses, for purely administrative reasons, counts of licensed vehicles at Local Taxation Offices included any vehicle licensed for at least one month during the third quarter of the year.

2.5 Secondly, the DVLA-based censuses relied on a complete count of all vehicles, subject only to the complexities of establishing accurately the licensing status of the vehicle, whereas before 1978, information on vehicle stock had been obtained mainly from a sample.

Taxation class changes

2.6 There have been two major changes in recent years. Firstly, as from 1 October 1982, all general goods vehicles less than 1,525 kgs unladen weight were assessed for vehicle excise duty at the same rate as private vehicles, and the old 'private car and van' taxation class was replaced by the new 'Private and Light Goods' (PLG) taxation class. In addition, goods vehicles greater than 1,525 kgs unladen weight were to be taxed with reference to their gross vehicle weight and axle configuration, as opposed to unladen weight as in previous years. Farmers' light goods vehicles and showmen's light goods vehicles, ie. vehicles of less than 1,525 kgs unladen weight, were allocated to their own distinct taxation classes and were not included in the PLG taxation class.

2.7 Secondly, as from 1 October 1990, goods vehicles less than 3,500 kgs gross vehicle weight were transferred from the 'Goods Vehicle' taxation class to the 'Private and Light Goods' class. Farmers' and showmen's goods vehicles of less than 3,500 kgs gross vehicle weight, but more than 1,525 kgs unladen weight, were transferred to the 'Light Goods Farmers' and 'Light Goods Showmen's' taxation classes.

Correction for taxation class changes

2.8 The changes described above created discontinuities in the time series for vehicles currently licensed. To correct for these discontinuities, retrospective estimates of 'Private and Light Goods' and 'Goods' have been made for the years before 1991 using the assumption that all general goods vehicles of less than 3,500kgs gross vehicle weight would have been taxed as 'Private and Light Goods'. Private cars taxed within 'Private and Light Goods' have been estimated pro-rata on the basis of information on the proportion of cars within 'Private and Light Goods' available for the first time in 1983.

2.9 Between 1978 and 1982, the distribution of private cars, within 'Private and Light Goods', by engine capacity has been estimated pro-rata by allocating retrospective estimates for total private cars within 'Private and Light Goods' across previous distributions of 'private cars and vans' by engine capacity.

2.10 As mentioned above, since October 1982 gross vehicle weight has been the basis of taxation for goods vehicles. Analyses of the stock of goods vehicles by gross weight have been compiled since the 1983 census. Pre-1983 time series analysed by gross vehicle weight are not available.

Regional analysis

2.11 The only regional information easily obtainable from vehicle records held on computer by DVLA is the post code of the registered keeper of the vehicle. This can be used to determine the county in which the keeper lives. The county and regional analyses throughout this report have been compiled in this way. Vehicles under disposal are those where the previous owner has sold the vehicle and notified DVLA, but the new keeper has not completed and returned his part of the registration document. For such vehicles the post code of the registered keeper is unknown.

3. NOTES ON VEHICLES REGISTERED FOR THE 1ST TIME: TABLES 10 to 13

Sources

3.1 The statistics in this section are based on a complete analysis of new registrations and not on a sample count. Monthly analyses are compiled from the records of the Driver and Vehicle Licensing Agency (DVLA) by the Department of Transport's DVOIT Agency.

Correction for taxation class changes

3.2 To correct for taxation class changes, as described under sections 3.6 and 3.7 above, retrospective estimates of 'Private and Light Goods' and 'General Goods' were made for 1969 to 1982 by assuming that all 'general goods' vehicles less than 1,525 kgs unladen vehicle weight would have been registered as PLG prior to 1 October 1982, if that taxation class had been in operation. A second set of retrospective estimates was made for 1980 to 1990 assuming that general goods vehicles of less than 3,500 kgs gross weight would have been registered as PLG.

3.3 From 1975 onwards, estimates have been made of the number of private cars taxed within the 'Private and Light Goods' class. Up to 1982 general goods vehicles and farmers' goods were taxed on their unladen weight and analyses were produced on this basis. Since 1983 gross vehicle weight has been the basis of taxation and new registrations have been analysed by gross vehicle weight.

4. NOTES ON HISTORIC SERIES: TABLES 9 AND 14

Motor vehicles currently licensed: census methods

4.1 Up to 1974, the figures for motor vehicles currently licensed were compiled from information received by the Department of Transport from all registration/licensing authorities or Local Taxation Offices (County, County Borough and Borough Councils) in Great Britain which administered the Vehicles (Excise) Act 1971.

4.2 Since October 1974, all new vehicles have been registered at the Driver and Vehicle Licensing Agency (DVLA), and records for older vehicles have also been transferred there, the process being completed in March 1978. For 1975 and 1976 the census was based on a combination of records held at Local Taxation Offices and at DVLA. Because of the closure of Local Taxation Offices it was not possible to produce census results in 1977. This system was superseded by censuses based entirely on the record of licensed vehicles at DVLA on 31 December 1978. Differences between censuses based entirely on DVLA records and those prior to 1978 are described in sections 3.4 and 3.5.

4.3 These differences meant that there was a discontinuity in the stock figures in 1978. Pre-1978 figures have therefore been adjusted to make them broadly comparable with those for subsequent years. These adjustments have been applied after the estimation described under 'correction for taxation class changes'.

Correction for taxation class changes

4.4 The changes described above under 3.6 and 3.7 created a discontinuity in the time series for vehicles currently licensed. To correct for this discontinuity, retrospective estimates of 'Private and Light Goods' and 'Goods' have been made for the years 1950 to 1982, using the assumption that all general goods vehicles of less than 3,500kgs gross vehicle weight would have been taxed as 'Private and Light Goods' if this class had existed prior to 1983. Private cars taxed within 'Private and Light Goods' have been estimated pro-rata on the basis of information on the proportion of cars within 'Private and Light Goods' available for the first time in 1983.

4.5 The 'Goods' category retains farmers' goods vehicles and showmen's goods vehicles of less than 1,525kgs unladen weight. From 1983, retrospective counts of vehicles within the new taxation class groupings were produced. Other taxation classes were unaffected by the change in goods vehicle taxation.

Motor vehicles registered for the first time

4.6 Statistics in this table are based on a complete analysis of new registrations and not on a sample count. In the past these were obtained from monthly returns of licensing authorities' records of new registrations. On 1 October 1974 the Driver and Vehicle Licensing Centre (DVLC) at Swansea took over responsibility for the licensing of vehicles from Local Taxation Offices (LTO). Initially, DVLC dealt only with new registrations, but from 1 April 1975 they began to take on the registration of older vehicles from the Local Vehicle Licensing Offices, which replaced the LTOs. On 1 April 1990, DVLC became the Driver and Vehicle Licensing Agency (DVLA).

Correction for taxation class changes

4.7 To correct for taxation class changes, retrospective estimates of 'Private and Light Goods' and 'General Goods' have been made for 1951 to 1982 by assuming that all 'general goods' vehicles less than 3,500kgs gross vehicle weight would have been registered as 'Private and Light Goods' prior to 1 October 1982, if that taxation class had been in operation. The 'Goods Vehicles' taxation class retains farmers' goods vehicles and showmen's goods vehicles less than 1,525kgs unladen weight. From 1975 onwards, estimates have been made of the number of private cars taxed within the 'Private and Light Goods' class. Other taxation classes were unaffected by the change in goods vehicle taxation.

5. NOTES ON GOODS VEHICLE STATISTICS: TABLES 18 TO 27

5.1 The purpose of tables 18 to 27 is to provide detailed information on heavy goods vehicles in terms of their GVW and axle configuration. This population of vehicles amounts to some 411,000 vehicles, compared with 428,000 vehicles in goods vehicle taxation groups.

Goods vehicles statistics in this publication

5.2 The goods vehicle statistics provided in tables 18 onwards cover those goods vehicles over 3.5 tonnes gross vehicle weight (GVW), in taxation groups 1 - 9, that is HGV, trailer

HGV and restricted HGV taxation groups for general goods, showman's goods and farmer's goods and taxation group 26 - goods (electric). In addition, results include vehicles in taxation group 60, crown vehicles, and groups 65 - 90, vehicles with various forms of exemption, provided they exceed 3.5 tonnes gross vehicle weight and have goods vehicle body type. Further information on taxation groups is given in table 3.

Goods vehicle statistics in earlier publications

5.3 Previous publications of 'Goods Vehicles In Great Britain' were based primarily on results taken from the Goods Vehicle List (GVL), a register of vehicles over 3.5 tonnes gross weight licensed to carry goods on the public road network, and maintained by the DVLA. This list is a count of goods vehicles (greater than 3.5 tonnes gross weight) designed to provide a sampling population for the Continuing Survey of Road Goods Transport (CSRGT). However, some tables in that publication were drawn from the 'Goods Vehicle Census', as described below.

5.4 Following the Armitage inquiry, the maximum weight limit for articulated vehicles was increased from 32.5 tonnes gross vehicle weight (GVW) to 38 tonnes GVW, effective from 1 May 1983. To monitor the effect of this change the Goods Vehicle Census, a new source of information on goods vehicles greater than 3.5 tonnes GVW and 1,525kgs unladen weight (ULW), was developed based on the DVLA register. It was designed to produce detailed information on heavy goods vehicles in terms of their GVW and axle configuration. This census included goods vehicles in a wider range of tax classes than the Goods Vehicle List, including certain goods vehicles in exempt classes.

5.5 Earlier editions of 'Goods Vehicles In Great Britain' explained how it was possible to reconcile the alternative estimates of goods vehicle stock provided by the two sources. After allowing for the differences in coverage the two estimates are close, the differences being attributable to the timing of the counts. The Goods Vehicle Census is taken six weeks after the end of the year census day to allow for the processing lag between application for licence and entry into the register. The GVL counts are taken on the last day of each calendar quarter since timely counts are needed for the CSRGT. Because of its use in sampling active vehicles the GVL contains recently unlicensed vehicles which may be in the process of relicensing.

Location of goods vehicle tables in earlier publications

5.6 Many of the tables in this report taken from 'Goods Vehicles in Great Britain' (GVGB), have been re-set to take less room and provide improved information. To assist readers who wish to compare tables 18 to 27 with earlier published information, the following schedule shows how the tables in this publication relate to the 1992 edition of 'Goods Vehicles in Great Britain'.

GVGB: 1992 edition	VLS: 1993 edition	Notes
Table 1	Table 18	
Trailer analysis	Trailer analysis	

16

Tables 2, 3 and 4	Table 21	Table 21 is further improved by the inclusion of more body type descriptions than previously.
Tables 5, 6 and 7	Table 22	
Tables 8, 9 and 10	Table 23	Table 23 is further improved by the inclusion of more body type descriptions than previously.
Tables 11 to 16	Table 24	In place of analyses based around traffic area offices, Table 24 provides the added detail of a breakdown of goods vehicles by county.
Tables 17, 18 and 19	Table 25	
Tables 21, 22 and 23	Table 26	
Table 24 and 26	Table 27	
Table 25	Table 19	Table 19 is improved to include rigid vehicles in addition to the articulated vehicles shown in the old table 25.
-	Table 20	A new analysis showing a breakdown of vehicles by axle configuration and by the taxation group in which they fall

6. TAXATION CLASS DEFINITIONS

6.1 In general the classes of vehicle are based on the taxation classes set out in schedules to the Vehicle (Excise) Act 1971, although in some cases they have been renamed.

Agricultural tractors and machinery

6.2 Agricultural tractors and other self propelled agricultural machinery which are used for certain defined purposes connected with agriculture and forestry are all taxed at a special rate £30 per annum at the end of December 1993. This taxation class also includes machinery, works trucks, mobile cranes and mowing machines which make little use of public roads.

Crown vehicle scheme

6.3 All vehicles owned by Government Departments apart from those belonging to the Armed Forces are registered but pay no tax under the Vehicles (Excise) Act. Most of these operate under Certificates of Crown ownership.

Farmer's goods vehicles

6.4 Vehicles registered in the name of a person engaged in agriculture and used on roads solely for the conveyance of the produce of, and requisites for, his agricultural land.

General haulage and showmen's tractors

6.5 A general haulage tractor is used for general haulage on the public highway; it may not be used for transporting goods except on the trailer which it is towing. A similar definition applies to showmen's tractors but with the added proviso that they may be used only for towing showmen's equipment.

Goods vehicles

6.6 Mostly goods vehicles over 3,500kgs gross vehicle weight but this category also includes farmers' and showmen's goods vehicles (see below) that are less than 3,500kgs.

Motorcycles, scooters and mopeds

6.7 No distinction between these different types of machine is made for taxation purposes. It is not possible to distinguish between motor scooters and motorcycles, and although many vehicles in the size category not over 50cc are mopeds, this is only a rough guide. Furthermore, from 1965, machines used with a sidecar cannot be distinguished since they are now subject to the same rates of tax as for solo machines.

Exempt vehicles

6.8 There are some vehicles designed and used for particular purposes which are registered when they are first brought into use but which pay no vehicle excise duty. Amongst these, three types (fire appliances, ambulances and road rollers) do not carry a licence disc and their exemption is indefinite without renewal. Others (eg invalid vehicles, snow ploughs, certain road construction vehicles) have their exemption from duty renewed annually and carry a licence disc.

6.9 The exempt vehicle statistics exclude cars and motor cycles used temporarily in Great Britain before being privately exported under the personal export and direct export schemes by non-United Kingdom citizens. Electric vehicles have been exempt from taxation since April 1980, and are included in the exempt vehicle statistics.

6.10 Since 1979 the figures include two classes of exempt vehicles which were not previously included; vehicles which make no use of public roads (tax class 61) and vehicles which make limited use of public roads (tax class 62).

Private and light goods

6.11 Includes all vehicles used privately. Mostly consists of private cars (whether owned by individuals or companies) and vans. However, from 1 October 1990, goods vehicles less than 3,500kgs gross vehicle weight are now included in this category.

Public transport vehicles

6.12 All vehicles classified for taxation purposes as hackneys; these are vehicles used for public conveyance, ie buses, coaches, taxis and private hire cars. Most of these with a seating capacity of not more than 8 persons are taxis and private hire cars. Buses and coaches not licensed for public conveyance, and operated and used privately, are excluded and are classified for excise licensing with private and light goods.

Three wheelers

6.13 Mainly three-wheeled cars and vans not exceeding 450kgs unladen weight. Motorised tricycles are also included but motorcycle combinations are included with motor cycles.

Trade licences

6.14 These are issued to manufacturers and repairers of, and dealers in, motor vehicles but as they do not relate to particular vehicles they are not included in any of the tables relating to current licences or new registrations.

Vehicles owned by the Armed Forces

6.15 Vehicles officially belonging to the Armed Forces, except for a small number which for particular reasons, are licensed in the ordinary way, operate under a special registration and licensing system operated by them. Such vehicles are excluded from vehicle registration figures.

Vehicles which make limited use of public roads (tax class 62)

6.16 Vehicles which use the public roads solely for moving from one part of the owner's property to another, to an extent not exceeding 6 miles in any week, are exempted from vehicle excise on an annual basis. They have to be registered when first brought into use, but they do not carry licence discs. This exempt class has been included in the figures for 'Other exempt vehicles' from 1979.

Vehicles which make no use of public roads (tax class 61)

6.17 Vehicles which are never used on public roads, that is on roads repairable at public expense, are not required to be registered unless the private roads on which they are used are roads to which the public have access (eg roads within railway termini). This exempt class has been included in the figures for 'Other exempt vehicles' from 1979.

Symbols and conventions

.. = not available
- = negligible (less than half the final digit shown)
0 = nil (where the quantity is known to be zero)
| = change or break in the series (cf table 16)

Table 1 Motor vehicles currently licensed: by taxation group: 1983-1993

Thousands

Year	Private and light goods [1] Body type cars	Other vehicles	Motor cycles scooters and mopeds	Public transport vehicles [2]	Goods [3,4]	Agricultural tractors etc [5]	Other vehicles [6]	Crown and exempt vehicles [7]	All vehicles	of which body type cars All	Per cent company
1983	15,543	1,692	1,290	113	488	376	86	621 [8]	20,209	15,852	11.6
1984	16,055	1,752	1,225	116	490	375	82	670	20,765	16,399	11.7
1985	16,454	1,805	1,148	120	485	374	78	695	21,159	16,829	11.8
1986	16,981	1,880	1,065	125	484	371	73	720	21,699	17,389	11.7
1987	17,421	1,952	978	129	485	374	68	744	22,152	17,856	12.2
1988	18,432	2,096	912	132	502	383	83	761	23,302	18,888	12.7
1989	19,248	2,199	875	122	505	384	77	785	24,196	19,720	13.0
1990	19,742	2,247	833	115	482	375	71	807	24,673	20,230	12.9
1991	19,737	2,215	750	109	449	346	65	840	24,511	20,253	12.0
1992 [10]	20,116	2,228	688	108	437	324	59	891	24,851	20,681	11.2
1992 [11]	19,870	2,198	684	107	432	324	59	903	24,577	20,444	11.1
1993	20,102	2,187	650	107	428	318	55	979	24,826	20,755	10.7

1 For years up to 1991 retrospective counts within these new taxation
   classes have been estimated. See notes and definitons on taxation class changes.
2 Includes taxis.
3 Includes agricultural vans and lorries
4 Excludes electric goods vehicles which are now exempt from licence duty.
5 Includes combine harvesters, mowing machines, digging machines,
   mobile cranes and works trucks.
6 Includes three wheelers, showmen's haulage and recovery vehicles.
7 Includes electric vehicles which are now exempt from licence duty.
8 Includes old vehicles exempt from tax converted for the first time to the DVLA system.
9 The above table relates to vehicles licensed in Great Britain. The equivalant figures for
   Northern Ireland are given in Northern Ireland Department of Environment
   publication "Transport Statistics". (N.B. In 1992 578,000 vehicles were licensed in
   Northern Ireland of which 493,000 were body type cars.)
10 For the years up to 1992 estimates are taken from the annual vehicle census based on the DVLA
   main vehicle file.
11 From 1992 estimates of licensed stock are taken from the Department of Transport's
   Statistics Directorate Vehicle Information Database. SEE TEXT

Table 2 Motor vehicles currently licensed: by taxation group, vehicle details: 1983-93

(a) Private and light goods: Body type cars within private and light goods by engine size   Thousands

Over	Not over	1983	1984	1985	1986	1987	1988	1989	1990	1991	1992	1992	1993
	700cc	132	128	123	120	114	108	99	90	79	71	70	62
700cc	1,000cc	1,754	1,832	1,891	1,963	2,022	2,145	2,205	2,215	2,163	2,109	2,084	1,998
1,000cc	1,200cc	2,075	2,109	2,128	2,153	2,154	2,201	2,215	2,226	2,198	2,232	2,207	2,227
1,200cc	1,500cc	4,936	5,043	5,076	5,115	5,111	5,259	5,361	5,418	5,358	5,411	5,349	5,330
1,500cc	1,800cc	3,813	4,030	4,278	4,573	4,850	5,279	5,641	5,872	5,944	6,105	6,025	6,129
1,800cc	2,000cc	1,488	1,524	1,556	1,616	1,718	1,920	2,162	2,352	2,465	2,655	2,622	2,841
2,000cc	2,500cc	621	650	665	694	710	736	747	744	726	727	719	722
2,500cc	3,000cc	412	428	433	445	448	476	501	509	498	496	489	482
3,000cc		308	308	301	301	294	307	314	315	306	309	305	312
cc not known[2]		4	3	2	1	1	1	1	1	1	-	-	-
All capacities		15,543	16,055	16,454	16,981	17,421	18,432	19,248	19,742	19,740	20,116	19,870	20,102
Other vehicles		1,692	1,752	1,805	1,880	1,952	2,095	2,199	2,247	2,215	2,230	2,198	2,187
All private and light goods[3]		17,235	17,807	18,259	18,259	19,374	20,528	21,447	21,989	21,952	22,345	22,069	22,289

(b) Motor cycles, scooters and mopeds: by engine size   Thousands

Over	Not over	1983	1984	1985	1986	1987	1988	1989	1990	1991	1992	1992	1993
	50cc	474	449	423	389	352	312	280	248	207	174	173	147
50cc	125cc	432	425	402	377	347	320	303	284	249	221	222	204
125cc	150cc	10	8	6	5	4	3	3	3	2	2	2	2
150cc	200cc	74	63	54	45	39	34	31	28	24	21	22	19
200cc	250cc	126	112	99	88	78	71	68	65	60	55	55	52
250cc	350cc	12	12	12	13	13	15	16	16	15	15	15	15
350cc	500cc	62	57	53	49	46	45	45	45	42	42	41	42
500cc		99	99	98	98	99	112	131	146	150	158	155	169
All over 50cc		816	776	725	676	626	600	595	587	543	514	512	503
All engine sizes		1,290	1,225	1,148	1,065	978	912	875	835	750	688	684	650

(c) Public transport vehicles: by seating capacity   Thousands

Over	Not over	1983	1984	1985	1986	1987	1988	1989	1990	1991	1992	1992	1993
	4 seats	36.8	40.2	43.7	47.0	47.7	46.7	35.3	26.8	21.5	18.1	18.0	15.4
4 seats	8 seats	9.0	9.1	9.3	9.6	10.5	13.0	14.0	15.0	16.1	17.1	17.0	17.9
All 8 seats or less		45.8	49.3	53.0	56.6	58.2	59.7	49.3	42.0	37.6	35.3	35.0	33.4
8 seats	32 seats	8.7	8.9	9.6	12.3	15.3	17.3	18.9	20.0	20.7	21.5	21.4	22.5
32 seats	48 seats	10.4	9.4	8.6	8.0	7.7	7.3	6.7	6.3	6.1	6.4	6.4	6.8
48 seats		48.4	48.7	48.6	48.0	47.9	48.2	47.3	46.2	44.8	44.6	44.4	43.9
All over 8 seats		67.5	67.0	66.8	68.4	70.8	72.8	72.9	72.5	71.5	72.5	72.2	73.3
All capacities		113.3	116.3	119.8	125.0	129.0	132.5	122.2	114.7	109.1	107.8	107.2	106.6

(d) General goods:by gross weight[4]   Thousands

Over	Not over	1983	1984	1985	1986	1987	1988	1989	1990	1991	1992	1992	1993
3.5 tonnes	7.5 tonnes	132	136	138	141	145	153	157	155	148	143	143	139
7.5 tonnes	12 tonnes	32	29	26	24	22	21	20	18	17	16	16	15
12 tonnes	25 tonnes	148	147	145	143	143	147	146	140	129	124	123	120
25 tonnes	33 tonnes	79	75	69	66	64	65	62	55	49	46	45	47
33 tonnes	38 tonnes	11	20	27	34	41	51	59	61	60	63	62	65
38 tonnes		1	-	-	-	-	-	-	-	-	-	-	-
Gross weight unknown		7	7	7	7	7	7	7	2	1	1	1	-
All vehicles		410	414	412	415	422	444	451	432	403	393	389	387

Table 2 (Continued)

(e) Farmers' goods: by gross weight[4]

Thousands

Over	Not over	1983	1984	1985	1986	1987	1988	1989	1990	1991	1992	1992	1993
	3.5 tonnes	3	3	3	22	21	19	18	20	20	19	19	19
3.5 tonnes	7.5 tonnes	8	8	8	8	7	7	7	7	7	7	7	6
7.5 tonnes	12 tonnes	3	3	2	2	2	2	2	1	1	1	1	1
12 tonnes	25 tonnes	7	7	7	7	6	6	5	4	5	5	5	4
25 tonnes	33 tonnes	2	2	2	1	1	1	1	1	1	1	1	1
33 tonnes	38 tonnes	-	-	-	-	-	-	-	1	1	1	1	1
38 tonnes		-	-	-	-	-	-	-	-	-	-	-	-
Gross weight unknown		55	53	51	28	25	23	20	14	12	10	10	8
All vehicles		78	76	73	68	62	58	54	48	46	43	43	41

(f) Agricultural tractors and machinery

Thousands

	1983	1984	1985	1986	1987	1988	1989	1990	1991	1992	1992	1993
Agricultural tractors	250	248	247	244	245	246	241	237	221	209	210	207
Combine harvesters and other agricultural machinery	41	41	42	42	42	43	43	44	41	40	40	40
Mowing machines	11	12	11	11	11	12	12	11	8	7	7	7
Digging machines	38	38	37	37	39	42	44	43	40	36	36	35
Mobile cranes	9	9	9	9	8	9	9	9	8	7	7	7
Works trucks	27	27	27	28	29	32	34	32	29	25	25	23
All vehicles	376	375	374	371	374	383	384	376	346	324	324	318

(g) Other licensed vehicles

Thousands

	1983	1984	1985	1986	1987	1988	1989	1990	1991	1992	1992	1993
Three wheelers less than 450 kgs	80	76	72	67	62	57	53	48	43	39	39	35
General haulage & showman's haulage	6	6	6	6	6	6	5	4	3	2	2	2
Others[5]	-	-	-	-	1	20	20	20	19	18	18	17
All vehicles	86	82	78	73	68	83	77	72	65	59	59	55

(g) Crown and other vehicles exempt from licence duty[6,7]

Thousands

	1983	1984	1985	1986	1987	1988	1989	1990	1991	1992	1992	1993
Crown vehicles	39	39	39	39	39	38	38	38	36	35	36	34
All other exempt vehicles	582	631	656	681	706	722	747	770	804	855	867	945
All exempt vehicles	621	670	695	721	744	761	785	808	840	891	903	979

1   Between 1978 and 1982 the distribution of cars within the 'Private
    and light goods' taxation class has been estimated. See notes and definitions.
2   Includes a small number of vehicles classified by horsepower.
3   Counts of vehicles in 'Private and light goods' have been estimated up to 1991.
    See notes and definitions.
4   Analyses by gross weight are only available from 1983. Analyses by unladen weight
    are available for previous years and were last published in Transport Statitics Great Britain 1975-1985.
5   From 1987 mainly recovery vehicles.
6   Includes electric vehicles which are now exempt from licence duty.
7   From 1983 includes a large number of old vehicles exempt from tax converted to the DVLA system.

23

Table 3 Motor vehicles currently licensed: by body type: 1983-1993

Thousands

Year	Cars	Taxis[1]	Motor cycles	Three Wheelers	Light Goods	Goods	Buses & Coaches	Agricultural tractors etc[2]	Other vehicles[3]	All vehicles
1983	15,852	24	1,399	74	1,509	635	148	344	222	20,209
1984	16,399	25	1,343	71	1,560	637	149	345	234	20,765
1985	16,829	25	1,262	62	1,606	633	148	344	248	21,157
1986	17,389	26	1,176	60	1,670	634	149	340	256	21,699
1987	17,856	28	1,086	57	1,732	636	150	340	267	22,152
1988	18,888	29	1,016	54	1,863	671	155	341	286	23,302
1989	19,720	30	976	51	1,956	674	156	334	298	24,196
1990	20,230	32	932	47	1,994	658	157	328	297	24,673
1991	20,253	32	848	43	1,961	624	154	309	287	24,511
1992 [4]	20,681	32	784	40	1,976	606	155	297	280	24,851
1992 [5]	20,444	32	780	40	1,951	600	154	298	280	24,577
1993	20,755	32	744	36	1,943	587	153	294	282	24,826

1 These include mainly custom built 'black cab' design vehicles.

2 Includes various types of harvesters, works trucks, mobile cranes and mowing machines.

3 Examples include ambulances, fire engines, road rollers, road construction vehicles, street cleansing etc etc.

4 For the years up to 1992 estimates are taken from the annual vehicle census based upon DVLA main vehicle file.

5 From 1992 estimates of licensed stock are taken from the Depatment of Transport's Statistics Directorate Vehicle Information Database.   SEE TEXT.

Table 4 Motor vehicles currently licensed 1993: by year of first registration

(a) Private and light goods: Body type cars within private and light goods: by engine size — Thousands

Over	Not over	Pre 1980	1980-81	1982-83	1984-85	1986-87	1988-89	1990-91	1992-93	All
	700cc	4.7	4.9	9.3	10.7	16.1	10.5	3.0	2.6	61.9
700cc	1,000cc	115.9	148.8	264.5	335.5	381.3	401.8	228.0	122.1	1,997.9
1,000cc	1,200cc	134.5	134.0	254.1	343.4	352.9	362.8	319.4	325.5	2,226.5
1,200cc	1,500cc	218.4	278.2	605.4	756.1	849.0	1,029.0	839.6	754.7	5,330.4
1,500cc	1,800cc	141.4	174.3	564.0	870.8	1,105.5	1,296.1	1,036.8	940.4	6,129.4
1,800cc	2,000cc	68.3	71.5	171.6	251.0	380.5	638.7	589.0	670.0	2,840.6
2,000cc	2,500cc	50.5	47.8	87.9	106.5	125.9	114.2	88.3	101.2	722.2
2,500cc	3,000cc	37.3	23.9	52.8	61.6	67.9	102.5	78.3	57.2	481.5
3,000cc		46.6	18.2	27.9	34.4	35.9	55.4	43.2	50.0	311.8
cc not known		-	-	-	-	-	-	-	-	-
All private cars		817.5	901.7	2,037.6	2,769.8	3,315.0	4,011.0	3,225.6	3,023.7	20,102.3

(b) Motor cycles, scooters and mopeds: by engine size — Thousands

Over	Not over	Pre 1980	1980-81	1982-83	1984-85	1986-87	1988-89	1990-91	1992-93	All
	50cc	9.4	13.8	22.9	25.6	22.9	21.8	18.2	12.2	146.7
50cc	125cc	16.1	14.8	25.4	31.3	30.2	33.3	30.4	22.1	203.6
125cc	150cc	1.0	0.2	0.1	0.1	0.1	0.1	0.1	0.1	1.7
150cc	200cc	6.2	5.6	2.1	1.2	0.5	1.3	1.3	1.0	19.4
200cc	250cc	9.7	14.8	6.6	2.1	2.4	4.6	5.9	6.2	52.4
250cc	350cc	2.2	0.9	0.8	1.2	2.2	2.3	2.4	2.9	15.0
350cc	500cc	9.6	6.2	4.9	3.0	2.9	3.3	5.1	7.2	42.2
500cc		18.1	10.4	10.1	11.8	13.8	24.8	36.0	43.8	168.8
All over 50cc		62.9	53.0	50.0	50.7	52.2	69.8	81.2	83.3	503.1
All engine sizes		72.3	66.8	72.9	76.3	75.0	91.6	99.4	95.5	649.8

(c) Public transport vehicles: by seating capacity — Thousands

Over	Not over	Pre 1980	1980-81	1982-83	1984-85	1986-87	1988-89	1990-91	1992-93	All
	4 seats	1.8	1.8	2.6	3.4	3.9	1.4	0.5	0.1	15.4
4 seats	8 seats	0.7	0.6	0.7	0.7	1.8	5.1	4.7	3.7	17.9
8 seats or less		2.5	2.4	3.3	4.1	5.6	6.4	5.1	3.8	33.4
8 seats	32 seats	0.5	0.6	0.9	1.9	6.5	5.3	3.7	3.2	22.5
32 seats	48 seats	2.5	0.6	0.5	0.4	0.3	0.5	0.7	1.4	6.8
48 seats		13.8	7.4	6.0	4.7	2.9	4.2	2.8	2.0	43.9
All over 8 seats		16.8	8.6	7.4	6.9	9.6	10.0	7.3	6.6	73.3
All capacities		19.3	11.0	10.7	11.1	15.3	16.4	12.4	10.5	106.6

(d) General goods vehicles: by gross weight — Thousands

Over	Not over	Pre 1980	1980-81	1982-83	1984-85	1986-87	1988-89	1990-91	1992-93	All
	3.5 tonnes	-	-	-	-	-	-	-	-	0.1
3.5 tonnes	7.5 tonnes	4.3	4.6	9.1	17.0	24.1	·35.5	25.0	20.0	139.5
7.5 tonnes	12 tonnes	0.8	0.5	0.9	1.8	2.9	3.3	2.6	2.4	15.2
12 tonnes	25 tonnes	3.1	3.1	7.9	15.9	22.8	32.4	19.9	14.4	119.5
25 tonnes	33 tonnes	1.3	1.0	2.5	5.0	8.5	13.5	7.5	8.1	47.4
33 tonnes	38 tonnes	0.4	0.5	2.3	6.8	11.0	19.5	11.1	13.5	65.3
38 tonnes		-	-	-	-	-	-	-	-	-
Gross weight unknown		0.3	-	-	-	-	0.1	-	-	0.5
All vehicles		10.2	9.8	22.8	46.5	69.3	104.3	66.1	58.4	387.4

Table 4 (Continued):

(e) Farmers goods vehicles: by gross weight

Over	Not over	Pre 1980	1980-81	1982-83	1984-85	1986-87	1988-89	1990-91	1992-93	All
	3.5 tonnes	2.3	2.0	2.0	3.5	3.3	3.3	1.9	1.0	19.3
3.5 tonnes	7.5 tonnes	1.6	0.8	0.9	1.2	0.9	0.6	0.2	0.1	6.3
7.5 tonnes	12 tonnes	0.3	0.1	0.2	0.2	0.1	0.1	-	-	1.1
12 tonnes	25 tonnes	0.6	0.5	0.8	1.0	0.7	0.5	0.2	0.1	4.4
25 tonnes	33 tonnes	0.1	0.1	0.1	0.2	0.1	0.1	0.1	0.0	0.9
33 tonnes	38 tonnes	-	-	0.1	0.1	0.1	0.2	0.1	0.1	0.6
38 tonnes		-	-	-	-	-	-	-	-	-
Gross weight unknown		3.2	0.4	1.8	1.4	0.8	0.6	0.2	-	8.4
All vehicles		8.2	3.8	5.9	7.5	6.2	5.3	2.7	1.4	40.9

(f) Agricultural tractors and machinery   Thousands

	Pre 1980	1980-81	1982-83	1984-85	1986-87	1988-89	1990-91	1992-93	All
Agricultural tractors	56.7	12.7	19.5	22.4	19.2	25.1	22.9	28.2	206.7
Combine harvesters etc	8.2	1.6	2.8	4.0	4.1	5.6	5.6	8.1	40.0
Mowing machines	0.2	0.1	0.2	0.4	0.8	1.5	1.8	2.0	6.9
Digging machines	4.3	1.3	2.1	2.9	4.3	7.9	5.6	6.1	34.5
Mobile cranes	2.4	0.5	0.4	0.5	0.5	1.2	0.7	0.4	6.5
Works trucks	2.1	0.9	1.4	2.1	3.1	6.7	3.6	3.4	23.3
All Vehicles	73.8	17.2	26.3	32.3	32.0	48.1	40.3	48.1	318.0

(g) Other licensed vehicles   Thousands

	Pre 1980	1980-81	1982-83	1984-85	1986-87	1988-89	1990-91	1992-93	All
Three wheelers less than 450kg	11.7	4.1	5.0	4.4	3.8	3.0	1.2	2.0	35.1
General haulage & showmens haulage	0.3	0.1	0.2	0.3	0.4	0.5	0.3	0.2	2.2
Others[1]	3.8	1.9	2.3	2.3	1.9	3.7	1.0	0.5	17.4
All Vehicles	15.7	6.1	7.5	7.0	6.1	7.2	2.5	2.7	54.7

1 From 1987 on, mainly recovery vehicles.

(h) Crown and other vehicles exempt from licence duty   Thousands

	Pre 1980	1980-81	1982-83	1984-85	1986-87	1988-89	1990-91	1992-93	All
Crown vehicles	6.3	1.4	1.8	3.2	3.9	5.0	5.9	6.2	34.1
All other exempt vehicles	259.2	40.7	78.0	93.8	87.5	99.9	106.0	171.6	945.1
All exempt vehicles	265.5	42.1	79.8	97.0	91.3	104.9	111.9	177.7	979.2

Table 5 Motor vehicles currently licensed 1993: by propulsion type

					Thousands
Taxation class:	Petrol	Diesel	Electric	Others[1]	All
Private and light goods	20,077.5	2,206.9	-	4.8	22,289.1
of which: body type cars	18,913.4	1,185.4	-	3.5	20,102.3
Motor cycles, scooters and mopeds	649.1	0.7	-	0.1	649.8
Farmers' goods vehicles	12.1	28.8	-	-	40.9
General goods vehicles	3.1	384.3	-	-	387.4
Public transport vehicles	6.6	100.0	-	-	106.6
Agricultural tractors and machinery	7.8	308.2	-	2.0	318.0
Other licensed vehicles	38.4	16.3	-	-	54.7
Exempt vehicles	778.9	168.7	28.5	3.1	979.2
All vehicles	21,573.5	3,213.8	28.5	10.0	24,825.9

1   Includes steam powered, gas and petrol/gas.

Table 6 Motorcars currently licensed: 1987, 1990, & 1993: age distribution of stock and vehicle survival rate [1]

Age of vehicle		1987		1990		1993	
Over	Not over	Currently licensed thousand	Survival rate percentage	Currently licensed thousand	Survival rate percentage	Currently licensed thousand	Survival rate percentage
	2 years	3,730	95.7	4,127	95.8	3,181	94.2
2 years	4 years	3,364	93.4	3,958	93.6	3,317	92.0
4 years	6 years	3,120	92.0	3,425	91.9	4,093	90.7
6 years	8 years	2,600	86.3	3,152	88.4	3,386	86.8
8 years	10 years	2,340	71.3	2,359	76.6	2,840	78.9
10 years	12 years	1,180	45.5	1,648	51.1	2,097	61.9
12 years	14 years	596	..	755	26.1	928	30.8
14 years		924	..	805	..	940	..
All ages [2]		17,856		20,230		20,755	

Thousands / percentage

1   Vehicles with car body types in all taxation classes.
2   For a small number of cars the age of the vehicle is unknown.

Table 7 Motorcars currently licensed:
by year of 1st registration and engine size: 1993 [1]

										Thousands

Body type cars classified
by cylinder capacity:

Over	Not over	Pre 1980	1980 & 1981	1982 & 1983	1984 & 1985	1986 & 1987	1988 & 1989	1990 & 1991	1992 & 1993	All Vehicles
	700cc	6	5	9	11	16	11	3	3	64
700cc	1,000cc	135	152	270	343	389	410	238	131	2069
1,000cc	1,200cc	148	137	259	350	360	371	340	365	2330
1,200cc	1,500cc	233	286	623	776	869	1052	868	827	5539
1,500cc	1,800cc	151	180	582	894	1130	1322	1059	966	6286
1,800cc	2,000cc	73	74	177	258	389	650	597	679	2897
2,000cc	2,500cc	58	50	91	110	129	116	89	103	746
2,500cc	3,000cc	43	25	55	63	69	104	79	58	496
3,000cc		55	19	29	35	37	56	44	51	326
cc not known		1	-	-	-	-	-	-	-	2
All body type cars		904	928	2097	2840	3386	4093	3317	3181	20755

1 Vehicles with car body types in all taxation classes.

Table 8 Motor vehicles currently licensed: by taxation group, county, region: 1993

Thousands

County Region Country	Private and light goods		Motor cycles scooters and mopeds	Public transport vehicles [1]	Goods [2,3]	Agricultural tractors etc [4]	Other vehicles [5]	Crown and exempt vehicles [6]	All vehicles	of which body type cars	
	Body type cars	Other vehicles								All	Percent co.
Cleveland	168.3	16.0	4.4	0.6	3.0	2.5	0.5	11.5	206.8	177.5	4.8
Cumbria	178.1	20.5	6.8	0.8	5.1	8.2	0.6	11.8	231.8	184.4	9.4
Durham	168.7	18.1	4.1	1.4	4.0	3.5	0.5	14.8	215.0	180.7	4.8
Northumberland	88.5	9.0	2.3	0.2	1.8	3.9	0.3	5.1	111.2	92.0	4.7
Tyne and Wear	280.8	28.3	4.6	2.4	5.2	1.9	0.7	18.6	342.6	296.0	8.9
Northern	884.3	91.9	22.2	5.4	19.1	19.9	2.7	61.7	1,107.3	930.6	7.0
Humberside	268.5	28.1	17.3	1.1	6.6	7.9	1.2	12.7	343.4	276.8	7.4
North Yorkshire	256.1	32.3	12.2	0.8	8.8	14.1	0.9	13.3	338.5	261.9	7.1
South Yorkshire	401.7	44.2	11.6	2.7	9.6	4.5	1.6	29.5	505.5	425.9	7.1
West Yorkshire	642.5	113.6	15.0	2.7	20.8	5.2	2.3	37.5	839.6	667.2	12.1
Yorks and H'side	1,568.8	218.1	56.2	7.4	45.7	31.7	6.0	93.0	2,026.9	1,631.8	9.2
Derbyshire	273.8	33.8	10.4	1.7	7.1	5.0	1.2	14.1	347.0	282.5	12.0
Leicestershire	314.0	33.9	10.6	1.4	6.4	4.5	1.1	13.0	384.8	322.0	11.2
Lincolnshire	223.9	27.4	10.3	0.9	6.7	15.8	1.0	14.1	300.0	231.2	7.1
Northamptonshire	212.7	22.2	7.3	1.0	6.8	3.2	0.6	9.6	263.4	217.8	11.8
Nottinghamshire	354.3	38.7	13.2	1.2	8.2	4.9	1.3	20.5	442.3	369.8	8.2
East Midlands	1,378.7	155.9	51.8	6.2	35.2	33.4	5.1	71.2	1,737.5	1,423.3	10.0
Cambridgeshire	275.5	33.4	12.0	1.0	6.7	8.9	0.8	12.5	350.8	281.8	11.1
Norfolk	304.2	36.6	16.3	1.2	6.4	12.3	1.1	14.6	392.7	311.7	9.3
Suffolk	255.9	28.2	14.0	0.7	7.2	7.9	0.9	12.2	327.0	262.5	6.8
East Anglia	835.7	98.2	42.3	2.9	20.3	29.1	2.8	39.3	1,070.6	856.1	9.1
Bedfordshire	211.3	22.6	6.1	1.0	3.7	2.8	0.4	7.8	255.8	215.6	11.8
Berkshire	379.2	35.7	9.6	1.0	5.4	2.4	0.6	9.2	443.1	384.2	20.3
Buckinghamshire	275.8	23.0	6.9	0.5	5.6	2.9	0.4	8.1	323.1	280.3	17.2
East Sussex	253.7	28.0	8.4	1.3	3.0	2.1	0.7	9.3	306.5	259.6	5.2
Essex	597.5	65.6	19.9	2.9	10.3	7.0	1.6	22.7	727.4	611.8	6.2
Greater London	2,260.8	219.6	63.6	21.9	33.6	4.9	3.5	65.9	2,673.7	2,302.3	16.3
Hampshire	642.2	64.3	26.1	1.4	8.5	6.3	1.6	26.0	776.4	655.0	8.5
Hertfordshire	479.2	47.8	13.1	1.9	8.7	4.1	0.9	13.5	569.2	486.8	12.8
Isle of Wight	46.4	5.7	2.8	0.2	0.5	0.7	0.2	2.1	58.6	47.7	2.8
Kent	586.6	62.1	23.0	2.2	9.5	7.5	2.0	23.8	716.7	600.1	7.1
Oxfordshire	227.3	24.2	10.4	0.8	4.0	4.1	0.6	7.6	279.0	231.2	8.1
Surrey	442.7	43.2	13.1	1.5	7.0	2.4	0.7	13.0	523.7	448.9	8.6
West Sussex	300.6	28.6	9.2	0.5	2.9	2.8	0.7	8.8	354.0	306.0	8.5
South East	6,703.4	670.4	212.2	37.1	102.7	49.9	13.8	217.9	8,007.2	6,829.4	12.1
Avon	373.7	40.1	16.7	1.6	8.2	2.9	1.1	12.8	457.1	381.3	10.2
Cornwall	175.2	23.7	9.5	1.0	3.3	6.6	0.8	10.7	230.8	181.3	3.8
Devonshire	384.4	49.0	19.7	2.1	6.7	11.2	1.4	17.7	492.2	395.0	5.2
Dorset	275.7	29.8	11.9	1.1	3.3	4.5	0.8	10.3	337.4	281.9	4.9
Gloucestershire	223.9	24.7	10.7	0.8	4.2	4.0	0.6	9.7	278.5	229.2	7.2
Somerset	185.8	22.4	8.8	0.7	6.7	6.7	0.6	8.8	240.5	190.2	5.2
Wiltshire	284.3	28.1	11.1	0.7	6.4	5.2	0.7	10.4	346.8	289.3	23.9
South West	1,903.0	217.9	88.5	7.8	38.7	41.1	6.0	80.4	2,383.4	1,948.1	9.0
Hereford & Worcs	278.4	32.4	10.3	1.0	6.6	7.4	0.8	12.4	349.3	285.3	12.5
Salop	163.7	20.4	5.4	0.5	6.2	7.1	0.5	10.8	214.7	169.0	8.8
Staffordshire	351.9	36.9	12.9	1.9	8.8	5.6	1.4	19.8	439.0	366.8	7.0
Warwickshire	202.6	18.9	6.7	0.7	4.0	3.7	0.5	8.4	245.6	207.4	20.9
West Midlands	1,006.9	105.4	20.9	4.1	27.0	4.1	2.9	43.5	1,214.8	1,038.6	20.1
West Midlands	2,003.5	214.0	56.2	8.2	52.6	27.8	6.2	95.0	2,463.4	2,067.2	15.9

29

Table 8 (Continued)

Thousands

County	Private and light goods		Motor cycles scooters and mopeds	Public transport vehicles [1]	Goods [2,3]	Agricultural tractors etc [4]	Other vehicles [5]	Crown and exempt vehicles [6]	All vehicles	of which body type cars	
	Body type cars	Other vehicles								All	Percent co.
Cheshire	358.4	37.5	12.5	1.3	8.7	5.4	0.9	19.1	443.7	373.0	7.0
Gtr Manchester	827.1	86.8	16.6	3.8	22.4	3.8	2.4	42.8	1,005.6	860.8	17.2
Lancashre	514.6	55.0	16.4	3.7	12.0	6.7	1.7	30.7	640.7	538.4	6.3
Merseyside	370.5	34.3	8.8	4.2	6.7	1.4	1.0	37.3	464.1	403.3	6.4
North Western	2,070.6	213.6	54.3	13.0	49.8	17.2	5.9	129.9	2,554.1	2,175.5	10.8
England	17,348.0	1,880.0	583.5	87.9	363.9	250.1	48.4	788.6	21,350.4	17,862.0	11.2
Borders	37.1	4.9	0.7	0.2	1.0	2.5	0.1	1.7	48.3	38.0	7.8
Central Scotland	95.5	9.3	1.4	0.4	2.4	1.5	0.2	5.2	115.9	99.7	20.4
Dumfries & Galloway	50.2	6.3	1.5	0.1	2.0	4.3	0.2	2.9	67.5	51.9	6.0
Fife	105.2	9.2	2.3	0.6	1.7	2.5	0.2	6.5	128.3	110.5	4.5
Grampain	186.1	20.3	4.5	1.1	5.3	9.3	0.4	7.2	234.0	189.6	8.3
Highland	66.6	10.1	1.9	0.4	1.8	3.3	0.2	3.8	88.0	68.5	5.4
Lothian	236.3	23.4	3.9	2.5	4.1	2.9	0.4	15.4	288.9	245.0	15.2
Orkney	6.9	1.3	0.3	0.1	0.3	1.2	0.0	0.6	10.6	7.1	5.3
Shetland	7.7	1.8	0.3	0.1	0.3	0.5	0.0	0.5	11.3	7.9	6.6
Strathclyde	578.1	55.2	6.6	5.7	13.1	8.0	0.9	44.7	712.2	616.4	8.8
Tayside	126.7	13.0	2.5	0.6	2.9	5.7	0.3	6.1	157.8	130.6	7.3
Western Isles	7.9	1.6	0.1	0.1	0.3	0.4	0.0	0.4	11.0	8.2	4.0
Scotland	1,504.3	156.5	25.9	11.9	35.3	42.0	2.8	95.1	1,873.8	1,573.5	9.7
Clwyd	143.9	16.0	4.5	0.5	3.6	3.3	0.4	10.8	183.0	152.3	4.5
Dyfed	123.0	18.1	3.4	0.8	4.7	6.0	0.4	11.9	168.2	130.1	3.3
Gwent	149.2	16.3	4.3	1.0	3.3	1.8	0.4	12.2	188.5	159.6	5.3
Gwynedd	82.9	11.8	2.3	0.8	2.4	3.1	0.2	5.9	109.4	86.8	3.1
Mid Glamorgan	141.3	15.0	3.0	0.9	2.7	1.0	0.4	16.0	180.4	156.0	3.9
Powys	41.8	7.9	1.2	0.2	2.6	4.1	0.2	3.4	61.3	43.1	5.3
South Glamorgan	116.7	11.2	1.8	0.5	2.2	0.5	0.2	5.6	138.8	120.9	20.7
West Glamorgan	116.5	11.3	3.0	1.0	1.7	0.7	0.3	10.1	144.4	125.2	5.8
Wales	915.1	107.5	23.5	5.6	23.2	20.5	2.4	76.1	1,174.0	974.0	6.5
County unknown	35.2	3.2	1.0	0.1	0.5	0.4	0.1	1.8	42.2	36.6	4.7
No current keeper vehicle under disposal	299.8	39.6	15.8	1.1	5.4	4.9	1.0	17.7	385.4	308.9	0.0
Great Britain	20,102.3	2,186.8	649.8	106.6	428.4	318.0	54.7	979.2	24,825.9	20,755.0	10.7

1 Includes taxis.
2 Includes agricultural vans and lorries
3 Excludes electric goods vehicles which are now exempt from licence duty.
4 Includes combine harvesters, mowing machines, digging machines, mobile cranes and works trucks.
5 Includes three wheelers, showmen's haulage and recovery vehicles.
6 Includes electric vehicles which are now exempt from licence duty.

Table 9 Motor vehicles currently licensed: [1] 1903-1982

For greater detail of the years 1983-1993 see table 1

Thousands

Year	Private and light goods [2]		Goods [3,4]	Motor cycles etc [5]	Public transport vehicles [6]	Agricultural tractors etc [7]	Other vehicles [8]	Crown and exempt vehicles [9]	All vehicles
	Private cars	Other vehicles							
1903	8		4	..	5	..	..	..	17
1909	53		30	36	24	..	..	..	143
1920	187		101	228	75	..	..	..	591
1930	1,056		349	712	101	15	15	24	2,272
1939	2,034		488	418	90	31	3	84	3,148
1946	1,770		560	449	105	146	16	61	3,107
1950	1,979	439	439	643	123	262	24	61	3,970
1951	2,095	457	451	725	123	250	26	63	4,190
1952	2,221	477	450	812	119	270	29	86	4,464
1953	2,446	516	446	889	105	289	30	88	4,809
1954	2,733	566	450	977	97	307	32	88	5,250
1955	3,109	633	462	1,076	92	326	35	89	5,822
1956	3,437	685	471	1,137	89	336	37	95	6,287
1957	3,707	723	473	1,261	87	355	41	96	6,743
1958	4,047	772	461	1,300	86	367	46	96	7,175
1959	4,416	824	473	1,479	83	383	55	96	7,809
1960	4,900	894	493	1,583	84	392	65	101	8,512
1961	5,296	944	508	1,577	82	400	76	106	8,989
1962	5,776	1,002	512	1,567	84	401	83	107	9,532
1963	6,462	1,092	535	1,546	86	412	88	115	10,336
1964	7,190	1,184	551	1,534	86	421	90	120	11,176
1965	7,732	1,240	584	1,420	86	417	91	127	11,697
1966	8,210	1,283	577	1,239	85	399	87	142	12,022
1967	8,882	1,358	593	1,190	85	416	89	147	12,760
1968	9,285	1,388	580	1,082	89	409	92	157	13,082
1969	9,672	1,408	547	993	92	398	90	162	13,362
1970	9,971	1,421	545	923	93	385	89	121	13,548
1971	10,443	1,452	542	899	96	380	92	126	14,030
1972	11,006	1,498	525	866	95	371	95	128	14,584
1973	11,738	1,559	540	887	96	373	97	137	15,427
1974	11,917	1,547	539	918	96	380	96	149	15,642
1975	12,526	1,592	553	1,077	105	384	108	166	16,511
1976	13,184	1,626	563	1,175	110	387	117	156	17,318
1977	13,220	1,591	559	1,190	110	393	115	167	17,345
1978	13,626	1,597	549	1,194	110	394	111	177	17,758
1979	14,162	1,623	561	1,292	111	402	106	359	18,616
1980	14,660	1,641	507	1,372	110	397	100	412	19,199
1981	14,867	1,623	489	1,371	110	365	95	427	19,347
1982	15,264	1,624	477	1,370	111	371	91	454	19,762

1 The annual vehicle census of licensed vehicles has been taken as follows: 1903-1910 at 31 December; 1911-192 March; 1921-1925 for the highest quarter; 1926-1938 for the September quarter; 1939-1945 at 31 August; 1946- for the September quarter; 1977 census results are estimates; 1978-1991 at 31 December.

2 From 1950 onwards, retrospective counts within the October 1982 taxation classes have been estimated. For years up to 1990, retrospective counts within these new taxation classes have been estimated. See Notes on taxation class changes.

3 Includes agricultural vans and lorries, showmens' goods vehicles licensed to draw trailers (note 2 applies).

4 Excludes electric goods vehicles which are now exempt from licence duty.

5 Includes scooters and mopeds.

6 Includes taxis. Prior to 1969, tram cars were included.

7 Includes combine harvesters, mowing machines, digging machines, mobile cranes and works trucks.

8 Includes three-wheelers, showmens' haulage and recovery vehicles.

9 Includes electric vehicles which are now exempt from licence duty and personal and direct export vehicles.

Contact point for further information: 071-276 8208

Table 10 Motor vehicles registered for the first time: by taxation group: 1983-93

Thousands

Year	Private and light goods [1]		Motor cycles scooters and mopeds	Public transport vehicles [2]	Goods [3,4]	Agricultural tractors etc [5]	Other vehicles [6]	All vehicles	of which body type cars		
	Body type cars	Other vehicles							All	Per cent company	Per cent imports
1983	1,773.3	215.8	174.5	7.3	46.6	42.1	47.9	2,307.5	1,806.1	39	57
1984	1,721.6	211.0	145.2	7.2	49.6	40.1	64.2	2,238.9	1,759.3	42	57
1985	1,804.0	225.5	125.8	6.8	51.7	40.1	55.4	2,309.3	1,842.1	45	57
1986	1,839.3	231.4	106.4	8.9	51.4	34.8	61.5	2,333.7	1,883.2	46	54
1987	1,962.7	249.9	90.8	8.7	54.0	37.7	70.1	2,473.9	2,016.2	48	50
1988	2,154.7	282.3	90.1	9.2	63.4	45.2	78.6	2,723.5	2,210.3	51	55
1989	2,241.2	294.0	97.3	8.0	64.5	42.5	81.4	2,828.9	2,304.4	51	55
1990	1,942.3	237.6	94.4	7.4	44.4	34.2	78.4	2,438.7	2,005.1	52	56
1991	1,536.6	171.9	76.5	5.2	28.6	26.1	76.6	1,921.5	1,600.1	52	55
1992	1,528.0	166.4	65.6	5.1	28.7	24.1	83.9	1,901.8	1,599.1	52	55
1993	1,694.6	158.8	58.4	5.4	32.8	30.0	94.0	2,074.0	1,776.5	52	55

1 For years up to 1990 retrospective counts within these new taxation classes
   have been estimated. See notes and definitons on taxation class changes.
2 Includes taxis.
3 Includes agricultural vans and lorries and showman's goods vehicles
   licensed to draw trailers.
4 From 1981, excludes electric goods vehicles which are now exempt from licence duty.
5 Includes trench diggers, mobile cranes etc, but excludes agricultural tractors
   on exempt licences.
6 Includes Crown and exempt vehicles, three wheelers, pedestrian controlled
   vehicles, general haulage and showmen's tractors. From 1981 also includes
   electric goods vehicles which are now exempt from licence duty.
7 Cars in all taxation classes.

Contact point for
further information:
071-276 8208

Table 11 Motor vehicles registered for the first time: by taxation group, vehicle details: 1983-1993

(a) Private and light goods: by engine size

Thousands

Over	Not over	1983	1984	1985	1986	1987	1988	1989	1990	1991	1992	1993
	1,000cc	234.8	227.9	225.5	236.3	245.5	260.5	222.0	162.0	104.3	64.7	73.4
1,000cc	1,200cc	215.8	223.9	217.3	205.9	198.2	195.8	196.2	183.0	153.4	176.3	180.8
1,200cc	1,500cc	573.8	526.2	507.6	508.1	520.7	576.6	600.5	531.0	406.2	412.3	415.5
1,500cc	1,800cc	572.8	578.7	669.0	689.8	723.4	782.5	799.6	681.0	557.2	521.7	576.2
1,800cc	2,000cc	193.4	189.5	220.4	234.1	312.7	387.5	462.2	403.0	321.6	344.4	405.3
2,000cc	2,500cc	96.6	94.4	95.4	104.7	111.8	108.5	109.7	102.0	104.4	115.1	135.1
2,500cc	3,000cc	50.7	43.7	44.4	43.3	45.8	57.4	66.5	56.0	38.2	34.5	33.8
3,000cc		32.7	28.5	26.9	24.6	26.2	34.6	37.2	32.7	23.2	25.3	33.3
cc not known		0.5	0.4	0.4	0.3	0.1	0.1	0.1	0.1	0.1	0.1	0.1
All vehicles		1,970.0	1,913.2	2,006.9	2,047.2	2,184.3	2,403.6	2,494.0	2,151.7	1708.5	1694.2	1853.4

(b) Motor cycles, scooters and mopeds: by engine size

Thousands

Over	Not over	1983	1984	1985	1986	1987	1988	1989	1990	1991	1992	1993
	50cc	67.4	55.4	48.3	37.5	29.7	24.7	22.9	18.8	13.1	9.1	6.5
50cc	150cc	72.7	59.9	50.0	41.8	34.0	31.9	32.4	29.1	18.8	14.7	11.2
150cc	200cc	3.2	2.6	1.7	1.1	0.9	1.5	1.7	1.5	1.1	0.7	0.6
200cc	250cc	6.0	4.1	3.4	3.3	3.6	4.1	5.6	6.0	4.6	4.2	3.6
250cc	350cc	2.7	2.9	2.6	3.3	2.7	2.8	2.7	2.5	2.2	2.0	1.9
350cc	500cc	6.0	4.0	4.4	3.8	3.3	3.2	3.5	4.2	5.2	5.3	4.9
500cc		16.5	16.4	15.4	15.7	16.6	21.8	28.6	32.2	31.5	29.5	29.9
All vehicles		174.5	145.2	125.8	106.4	90.8	90.1	97.3	94.4	76.5	65.6	58.4

(c) Public transport vehicles: by seating capacity

Thousands

Over	Not over	1983	1984	1985	1986	1987	1988	1989	1990	1991	1992	1993
	4 seats	2.5	2.8	2.7	2.9	2.2	1.2	0.6	0.2	0.1	0.1	0.1
4 seats	8 seats	0.5	0.5	0.4	0.5	1.4	3.0	2.4	2.7	2.1	2.0	1.7
8 seats or less		3.0	3.3	3.1	3.4	3.6	4.2	3.0	2.9	2.2	2.0	1.8
8 seats	32 seats	0.7	0.7	1.3	3.5	3.6	2.7	2.4	2.5	1.6	1.6	1.7
32 seats	48 seats	0.3	0.2	0.3	0.2	0.2	0.2	0.3	0.5	0.3	0.4	0.8
48 seats		3.3	2.9	2.1	1.8	1.3	2.0	2.5	1.8	1.1	1.0	1.2
All over 8 seats		4.3	3.9	3.7	5.5	5.1	5.0	5.2	4.8	3.0	3.1	3.6
All capacities		7.3	7.2	6.8	8.9	8.7	9.2	8.2	7.7	5.2	5.1	5.4

(d) Goods: by gross weight

Thousands

Over	Not over	1988	1989	1990	1991	1992	1993
	3.5 tonnes	1.2	1.0	0.7	0.6	0.5	0.5
3.5 tonnes	7.5 tonnes	21.5	21.6	17.0	10.8	10.4	10.4
7.5 tonnes	12 tonnes	1.9	2.0	1.6	1.1	1.2	1.3
12 tonnes	25 tonnes	18.6	18.8	13.1	8.0	7.6	8.7
25 tonnes	33 tonnes	8.9	8.9'	4.8	3.1	3.2	3.9
33 tonnes	38 tonnes	11.3	12.2	7.2	5.0	5.9	8.1
38 tonnes		..	..	..	..	..	..
Gross weight unknown		-	-	-	-	-	-
All vehicles		63.4	64.5	44.4	28.6	28.7	32.8

Table 11 (Continued) Motor vehicles registered for the first time: by taxation group, vehicle details: 1983-1993

(e) Agricultural tractors and machinery   Thousands

	1983	1984	1985	1986	1987	1988	1989	1990	1991	1992	1993
Agricultural tractors	26.3	24.5	24.3	18.6	19.6	21.8	19.3	17.6	14.6	13.9	17.7
Combine harvesters and other agricultural machinery	3.2	3.3	3.7	2.6	2.7	3.0	3.0	2.8	2.4	2.5	2.5
Mowing machines	1.7	1.8	1.5	1.8	1.8	1.8	2.0	1.7	1.1	1.2	1.0
Digging machines	4.6	4.6	4.6	5.1	6.1	8.5	7.5	5.5	3.7	2.9	3.9
Mobile cranes	0.4	0.4	0.5	0.5	0.4	0.9	0.9	0.8	0.3	0.2	0.2
Works trucks	3.8	3.3	3.5	4.0	4.9	7.0	7.4	3.7	2.3	1.7	2.1
Others	2.2	2.2	2.1	2.2	2.2	2.3	2.4	2.2	1.7	1.8	2.6
All vehicles	42.1	40.1	40.1	34.8	37.7	45.2	42.6	34.2	26.1	24.1	30.0

(f) Other licenced vehicles   Thousands

	1983	1984	1985	1986	1987	1988	1989	1990	1991	1992	1993
Three wheelers and pedestrian controlled vehicles	3.2	2.9	2.6	2.6	2.2	2.1	1.5	1.2	0.3	1.2	1.0
General haulage and showman's haulage	0.6	0.4	0.4	0.4	0.4	0.4	0.2	0.1	0.1	0.1	0.1
Recovery vehicles [1]	.	.	.	.	.	0.9 [2]	0.9	0.7	0.4	0.3	0.3
All vehicles	3.8	3.3	3.0	3.0	2.6	3.4	2.6	2.1	0.7	1.6	1.4

(g) Crown and other vehicles exempt from licence duty   Thousands

	1983	1984	1985	1986	1987	1988	1989	1990	1991	1992	1993
Crown vehicles	5.0	5.1	5.8	5.3	4.6	4.1	4.4	4.0	3.2	3.7	3.1
Personal and direct export vehicles	7.9	8.2	9.2	9.3	10.8	9.9	9.9	9.1	8.9	7.1	7.5
Other exempt vehicles	31.2	47.6	37.5	44.0	52.2	56.1	64.4	63.1	63.8	71.6	81.9
All exempt vehicles	44.1	60.8	52.5	58.5	67.5	70.1	78.6	76.2	75.8	82.3	92.4

1 New tax class introduced in January 1988.
2 New tax class introduced in Jan 1988. Most registrations in 1988 were vehicles previously operated on trade plates. The figure shown for that year is an estimate of new registartions.

Contact point for
further information:
071-276 8208

Table 12 Motor vehicles registered for the first time: by county: 1993 with related information.

County Region Country	1983 All vehicles currently licensed (thousands)	1993 All Vehicles new registrations (thousands)	1993 All Vehicles currently licensed (thousands)	1993 Cars in all taxation classes new registrations (thousands)	1993 Cars in all taxation classes currently licensed (thousands)	1993 Cars in all taxation classes Per 1000 population [1]	1993 Cars in all taxation classes Average vehicle age
Cleveland	178	15.6	206.8	13.1	177.5	317	6.5
Cumbria	184	17.5	231.8	14.3	184.4	376	6.6
Durham	172	16.4	215.0	14.0	180.7	298	6.3
Northumberland	90	9.3	111.2	7.9	92.0	299	6.1
Tyne and Wear	285	31.6	342.6	27.7	296.0	261	6.1
Northern	909	90.3	1,107.3	77.1	930.6	300	6.3
Humberside	299	24.4	343.4	19.8	276.8	314	6.6
North Yorkshire	281	26.5	338.5	20.8	261.9	362	6.3
South Yorkshire	401	35.7	505.5	28.8	425.9	327	6.6
West Yorkshire	642	79.8	839.6	56.5	667.2	319	6.1
Yorks and H'side	1,623	166.4	2,026.9	125.9	1,631.8	326	6.3
Derbyshire	276	39.0	347.0	32.6	282.5	298	6.6
Leicestershire	325	48.6	384.8	43.5	322.0	357	6.8
Lincolnshire	254	18.8	300.0	14.6	231.2	387	6.9
Northamptonshire	208	19.5	263.4	15.2	217.8	369	6.6
Nottinghamshire	368	28.7	442.3	23.7	369.8	361	6.8
East Midlands	1,431	154.6	1,737.5	130.3	1,423.3	350	6.8
Cambridgeshire	269	32.3	350.8	26.4	281.8	416	6.7
Norfolk	326	25.9	392.7	21.3	311.7	409	7.1
Suffolk	271	21.7	327.0	17.3	262.5	405	7.2
East Anglia	866	80.0	1,070.6	65.0	856.1	410	7.0
Bedfordshire	218	20.0	255.8	17.2	215.6	402	6.7
Berkshire	337	52.2	443.1	47.3	384.2	507	6.1
Buckinghamshire	234	43.3	323.1	38.7	280.3	434	6.1
East Sussex	266	16.2	306.5	13.9	259.6	360	7.5
Essex	615	52.5	727.4	45.2	611.8	393	7.2
Greater London	2,493	273.1	2,673.7	244.8	2,302.3	333	6.9
Hampshire	630	54.9	776.4	47.5	655.0	413	7.2
Hertfordshire	488	61.9	569.2	56.1	486.8	490	6.5
Isle of Wight	50	2.6	58.6	2.3	47.7	380	8.2
Kent	605	44.2	716.7	37.4	600.1	390	7.2
Oxfordshire	235	18.1	279.0	14.9	231.2	394	7.0
Surrey	473	46.5	523.7	40.8	448.9	433	6.9
West Sussex	293	22.8	354.0	19.8	306.0	429	7.1
South East	6,937	708.3	8,007.2	625.9	6,829.4	386	6.9
Avon	401	11.1	457.1	9.6	381.3	394	7.3
Cornwall	194	11.5	230.8	9.4	181.3	381	7.8
Devonshire	408	26.1	492.2	21.0	395.0	378	7.6
Dorset	285	16.9	337.4	14.0	281.9	424	7.7
Gloucestershire	238	16.4	278.5	13.7	229.2	423	7.3
Somerset	203	11.5	240.5	8.7	190.2	403	7.7
Wiltshire	245	40.9	346.8	36.9	289.3	499	6.2
South West	1,974	134.2	2,383.4	113.3	1,948.1	410	7.3

Table 12 (Continued) Motor vehicles registered for the first time: by county: 1993: with related information.

County Region Country	1983 All vehicles currently licensed (thousands)	1993 All Vehicles		1993 Cars in all taxation classes			
		new registrations (thousands)	currently licensed (thousands)	new registrations (thousands)	currently licensed (thousands)	Per 1000 population [1]	Average vehicle age
Hereford & Worcs	272	29.0	349.3	25.1	285.3	413	6.9
Salop	164	14.7	214.7	11.8	169.0	410	6.9
Staffordshire	363	29.6	439.0	24.3	366.8	349	6.8
Warwickshire	171	26.9	245.6	24.0	207.4	422	6.2
West Midlands	962	145.4	1,214.8	129.6	1,038.6	395	6.2
West Midlands	1,932	245.8	2,463.4	214.8	2,067.2	392	6.5
Cheshire	355	36.1	443.7	30.0	373.0	386	6.5
Gtr Manchester	787	104.4	1,005.6	92.6	860.8	334	6.1
Lancashre	528	42.7	640.7	36.5	538.4	381	6.7
Merseyside	395	35.2	464.1	31.0	403.3	279	6.7
North Western	2,065	218.5	2,554.1	190.0	2,175.5	340	6.4
England	17,737	1798.0	21,350.4	1542.4	17,862.0	369	6.8
Clwyd	147	10.5	183.0	8.8	152.3	367	7.2
Dyfed	138	9.5	168.2	7.5	130.1	370	7.2
Gwent	155	12.0	188.5	10.1	159.6	355	6.9
Gwynedd	92	5.9	109.4	4.9	86.8	362	7.2
Mid Glamorgan	144	11.0	180.4	9.4	156.0	287	6.8
Powys	51	3.2	61.3	2.3	43.1	362	7.0
South Glamorgan	136	15.7	138.8	14.1	120.9	295	6.0
West Glamorgan	119	10.4	144.4	8.7	125.2	337	6.8
Wales	982	78.2	1,174.0	65.8	974.0	336	6.9
Borders	39	3.9	48.3	3.1	38.0	365	6.2
Central Scotland	80	11.8	115.9	10.3	99.7	367	5.5
Dumfries & Galloway	56	5.6	67.5	4.3	51.9	352	6.2
Fife	102	8.7	128.3	7.4	110.5	320	6.6
Grampain	182	19.5	234.0	15.9	189.6	369	6.0
Highland	68	7.1	88.0	5.6	68.5	335	6.2
Lothian	213	29.7	288.9	25.6	245.0	327	5.9
Orkney	9	0.5	10.6	0.3	7.1	368	7.3
Shetland	9	1.0	11.3	0.7	7.9	343	6.0
Strathclyde	553	70.2	712.2	61.9	616.4	268	5.7
Tayside	128	12.6	157.8	10.5	130.6	335	6.3
Western Isles	9	0.5	11.0	0.4	8.2	283	6.4
Scotland	1,448	171.0	1,873.8	146.0	1,573.5	308	5.9
County unknown	3	26.7	42.2	22.2	36.6	n/a	6.6
No current keeper vehicle under disposal	-	n/a	385.4	n/a	308.9	n/a	7.9
Great Britain	20,170	2074.0	24,825.9	1776.5	20,755.0	368	6.7

1 Based on 1992 provisional mid-year estimates of population.

Table 13 Monthly vehicle registrations: Seasonally adjusted series: 1988-1993 [1]

Thousands

Year	Month	Cars	Of which:- Imported	Company	Motor cycles	Goods	All vehicles
1988	Jan	181.2	98.1	91.0	7.5	5.0	227.6
	Feb	180.5	95.7	89.7	7.3	4.8	221.9
	Mar	165.9	97.6	91.4	7.5	5.1	219.2
	Apr	170.6	95.4	89.6	7.7	4.3	208.4
	May	190.1	101.9	94.0	7.7	5.5	231.7
	Jun	182.6	99.7	94.3	7.5	5.6	224.5
	Jul	186.8	99.8	95.8	7.4	5.2	228.9
	Aug	198.8	105.0	94.4	7.8	5.4	237.9
	Sep	203.8	103.4	102.8	6.5	5.9	246.3
	Oct	171.3	101.0	91.5	7.1	5.4	208.8
	Nov	185.9	104.9	96.4	7.9	5.6	230.2
	Dec	192.7	104.6	100.5	8.2	5.6	238.0
	All 1988	2210.3	1207.2	1131.4	90.1	63.4	2723.5
1989	Jan	193.4	101.8	97.2	8.3	6.3	237.1
	Feb	193.6	114.2	104.2	8.9	6.0	239.6
	Mar	194.9	103.0	98.6	8.1	5.3	238.4
	Apr	199.9	113.1	103.6	8.2	5.9	246.1
	May	195.0	108.1	101.0	8.3	6.1	240.6
	June	193.4	108.2	97.9	8.2	5.2	235.8
	July	188.0	104.0	94.1	7.9	5.3	229.7
	Aug	213.9	105.4	100.3	8.7	5.4	267.6
	Sept	175.1	101.9	90.6	8.0	6.0	218.5
	Oct	190.6	103.4	97.8	7.7	4.6	230.6
	Nov	183.6	103.8	94.5	7.5	4.4	222.7
	Dec	183.0	105.4	95.8	7.5	4.1	222.1
	All 1989	2304.4	1272.3	1175.5	97.3	64.7	2828.9
1990	Jan	184.4	105.8	93.5	8.4	4.5	232.2
	Feb	171.8	101.5	94.6	8.2	4.3	213.1
	Mar	175.1	102.6	93.2	8.6	3.9	220.3
	Apr	169.6	98.1	89.1	8.3	4.3	203.4
	May	181.7	98.9	91.1	8.6	3.8	220.7
	June	168.0	94.3	89.9	7.4	3.7	202.7
	July	165.0	91.6	89.0	7.6	3.7	203.7
	Aug	168.5	89.2	87.0	7.9	3.6	200.3
	Sept	166.8	88.7	85.4	7.3	3.6	197.5
	Oct	158.9	88.4	84.6	7.7	2.8	187.7
	Nov	151.1	82.9	80.9	7.4	3.0	181.4
	Dec	143.9	75.6	71.5	7.1	2.9	175.4
	All 1990	2005.1	1117.5	1049.9	94.4	44.0	2438.4
1991	Jan	146.3	78.5	74.5	7.6	2.8	184.3
	Feb	130.6	72.6	71.8	6.4	2.4	156.8
	Mar	149.4	80.3	76.2	7.3	2.5	181.1
	Apr	127.1	70.9	70.2	7.3	2.2	152.4
	May	126.2	71.2	68.3	6.8	2.4	153.7
	June	119.7	71.0	68.1	5.8	2.3	144.7
	July	129.6	74.6	73.0	6.1	2.2	160.9
	Aug	147.3	74.5	66.0	6.2	2.3	174.3
	Sept	139.9	73.7	70.1	5.8	2.4	162.9
	Oct	126.5	71.2	64.2	5.3	2.5	147.2
	Nov	129.3	69.2	66.3	6.0	2.3	151.5
	Dec	128.3	66.5	64.3	5.9	2.4	151.6
	All 1991	1600.1	874.2	833.1	76.5	28.6	1921.5
1992	Jan	129.4	68.5	69.5	6.1	2.3	154.7
	Feb	122.1	68.0	64.6	5.6	2.3	147.7
	Mar	123.9	68.9	63.4	5.4	2.5	149.1
	Apr	144.2	78.0	71.2	5.6	2.2	168.5
	May	130.0	72.9	68.2	5.8	2.1	156.6
	June	130.5	73.7	66.9	5.7	2.4	157.2
	July	128.0	70.9	66.4	5.8	2.7	151.7
	Aug	131.2	70.6	69.0	5.2	2.4	156.8
	Sept	130.6	70.8	66.9	4.6	2.3	153.8
	Oct	134.3	73.4	71.5	4.5	2.7	157.1
	Nov	133.3	72.5	69.3	4.5	2.5	157.4
	Dec	161.6	86.4	79.7	6.6	2.4	191.1
	All 1992	1599.1	874.5	826.7	65.6	28.7	1901.8
1993	Jan	136.2	76.1	67.6	5.4	2.2	161.9
	Feb	141.7	76.9	73.4	6.0	2.5	166.6
	Mar	140.0	76.8	74.1	5.6	2.1	164.2
	Apr	143.9	78.3	75.6	5.4	2.4	168.0
	May	146.6	81.0	77.6	5.4	2.5	172.0
	June	143.6	78.9	74.2	4.9	2.7	167.9
	July	147.0	83.3	72.6	4.7	2.5	168.6
	Aug	154.3	86.8	79.0	4.5	2.9	179.5
	Sept	150.6	86.5	77.6	4.0	4.2	176.4
	Oct	158.4	87.7	79.0	3.7	2.5	182.7
	Nov	161.7	91.6	81.3	4.3	3.2	188.1
	Dec	152.4	87.6	78.9	4.5	3.0	178.2
	All 1993	1776.5	991.5	910.1	58.4	32.8	2074.1

1. Seasonal adjustement constrained to equal actual annual totals.

Table 14 Motor Vehicles registered for the first time: 1951-1982

For greater detail of the years 1983-1993 see table 10

Thousands

Year	Private and light goods [1]	Goods vehicles [1]	Motor cycles etc [2]	Public transport vehicles [3]	Agri- cultural tractors etc [4]	Other vehicles [5,6]	All vehicles
1951	136.2	84.5	133.4	7.8	34.4	17.6	413.9
1952	187.6	81.8	132.5	5.4	35.3	16.0	458.6
1953	295.1	97.2	138.6	5.0	33.5	14.1	583.5
1954	386.4	109.6	164.6	5.5	35.2	17.1	718.4
1955	500.9	153.5	185.2	5.6	39.2	22.1	906.5
1956	399.7	148.0	142.8	5.1	31.9	23.3	750.8
1957	425.4	140.5	206.1	5.0	39.8	19.9	836.7
1958	555.3	172.6	182.7	4.9	47.2	18.9	981.6
1959	645.6	191.7	331.8	5.1	49.0	29.7	1,252.9
1960	805.0	225.9	256.7	6.4	42.5	32.9	1,369.4
1961	742.8	220.2	212.4	6.1	46.4	31.4	1,259.3
1962	784.7	192.3	140.2	5.5	42.8	26.7	1,192.2
1963	1,008.6	206.4	165.5	6.4	47.9	31.2	1,466.0
1964	1,190.6	229.3	205.1	6.5	46.1	33.6	1,711.2
1965	1,122.5	229.4	150.9	6.8	45.4	45.7	1,600.7
1966	1,065.4	227.2	109.4	6.8	48.4	36.4	1,493.6
1967	1,116.7	221.5	137.7	6.5	53.9	38.9	1,575.2
1968	1,116.9	231.7	112.0	7.1	57.0	37.2	1,561.9
1969	987.4	239.6	85.4	7.1	49.3	33.0	1,401.8
1969	1,133.2	93.8	85.4	7.1	49.3	33.0	1,401.8
1970	1,248.1	85.2	104.9	7.7	48.8	30.2	1,524.9
1971	1,462.1	74.2	127.9	9.5	37.9	30.0	1,741.6
1972	1,854.8	74.9	152.5	9.8	47.6	44.1	2,183.7
1973	1,851.3	82.7	193.6	10.0	49.7	43.0	2,230.3
1974	1,399.6	68.0	189.8	7.8	45.6	39.6	1,750.4
1975	1,317.2	67.0	264.8	7.8	48.5	44.6	1,749.9
1976	1,401.8	63.9	270.6	8.7	51.8	41.2	1,838.0
1977	1,445.0	68.8	251.3	8.8	48.3	39.8	1,862.0
1978	1,519.9	79.8	225.3	9.1	50.0	41.4	1,925.5
1979	1,891.5	91.3	285.9	9.1	47.7	44.4	2,369.9
1980	1,679.2	74.7	312.7	8.8	36.7	43.5	2,155.6
1980	1,699.2	54.9	312.7	8.8	36.7	43.5	2,155.8
1981	1,643.6	39.9	271.9	7.5	32.6	34.8	2,030.3
1982	1,745.5	41.2	231.6	7.1	41.2	39.6	2,103.9

1 From 1969 onwards registrations for the new October 1982 taxation classes have been estimated. See Notes. Figures for 1951- 1969 refer to previous classes. From 1980 onwards figures relate to the October 1990 taxation classes

2 Includes scooters and mopeds.

3 Includes taxis but excludes tram cars.

4 Includes trench diggers, mobile cranes, etc but excludes agricultural tractors on exempt licences.

5 Includes crown and exempt vehicles, three wheelers, pedestrian controlled vehicles, and showmens' goods vehicles.

6 Excludes vehicles officially registered by the armed forces.

Contact point for
further information:
071-276 8208

Table 15 International comparisons: Passenger vehicle stock: 1981 & 1991

Thousands

	Cars and taxis [1]		Motor cycles etc [2]		Buses and coaches		All passenger vehicles	
	1981	1991	1981	1991	1981	1991	1981	1991
Great Britain	15,451	21,029	1,503	794	74	78	17,028	21,901
Northern Ireland	371	486	15	11	2	2	388	499
United Kingdom	15,822	21,515	1,518	805	77	80	17,416	22,399
Belgium	3,206	3,970	514	438 [3]	17	14 [3]	3,737	4,423
Denmark	1,367	1,610 [3]	176	135 [3]	8	8 [3]	1,551	1,753
France	19,750 [5]	23,810 [3,5]	5,542 [5,6]	3,160 [3,5,6]	61	70	25,353	27,040
Germany [4]	26,543	36,515	4,063	3,685	123	133	30,729	40,333
Greece	911	1,777	130	296	19	21	1,059	2,095
Irish Republic	778	828	28	24	3	4	809	857
Italy	18,400	28,378 [3]	4,327	7,000 [3]	62	76 [3]	22,789	35,454
Luxembourg	133	192	2	4 [6]	1	1	136	196
Netherlands	4,600	5,569	765	640 [6]	12	12	5,376	6,222
Portugal	1,340	2,775	96	143 [6]	9	12	1,445	2,930
Spain	7,943	12,537	1,257 [6]	1,174 [6]	43	47	9,243	13,758
Austria	2,313	3,100	604	516	9	9	2,926	3,626
Czechoslovakia	2,216	3,342	670 [6]	557 [3,6]	32	40	2,918	3,940
Finland	1,279	1,923	221	62	9	9	1,509	1,994
Hungary	1,105	2,015	662 [6]	166 [6]	24	24	1,791	2,206
Norway	1,279	1,615	153	166	13	23	1,445	1,803
Sweden	2,893	3,619	16 [6]	45 [6]	13	15	2,922	3,679
Switzerland	2,394	3,066	840	750	12	14	3,246	3,829
Yugoslavia	2,568	..	162	..	26	..	2,756	..
Japan	24,612	37,076	13,091	17,295	231	248	37,934	54,620
USA	123,291	146,015	5,831	4,177	544	631	129,666	150,823

Note: These data conform to UN/ECE definitions of road vehicles.
1 Including car derived vans.
2 Includes mopeds and three-wheeled vehicles
3 Estimated from previous years.
4 Includes former Federal Republic of Germany and German Democratic Republic
5 Three-wheeled vehicles included under cars and taxis.
6 Excluding mopeds.

For futher details see 'International comparisons of Transport Statistics, Part 3: Road vehicles, traffic, and expenditure' published by HMSO, price £16.20.

Contact point for further information: 071-276-8515

Table 16 International comparisons: Passenger vehicles per head: 1981 & 1991

Vehicles per 1000 head of population

	Cars and taxis [1]		Motor cycles etc [2]		Buses and coaches		All vehicles	
	1981	1991	1981	1991	1981	1991	1981	1991
Great Britain	282	374	27.5	14.1	1.36	1.38	311	390
Northern Ireland	243	305	9.8	6.9	1.50	1.37	254	313
United Kingdom	281	372	27.0	13.9	1.36	1.38	309	388
Belgium	325	403	52.2	44.4	1.72	1.45	379	447
Denmark	267	313	34.4	26.2	1.49	1.58	303	341
France	367	416	102.9	55.2	1.13	1.22	471	473
Germany [4]	339	458	51.9	46.2	1.57	1.67	392	506
Greece	94	177	13.4	29.5	1.90	2.20	109	209
Irish Republic	226	236	8.2	7.0	0.82	1.25	235	245
Italy	322	491	75.7	121.1	1.09	1.32	399	614
Luxembourg	363	507	5.5	10.4	1.91	2.01	371	519
Netherlands	324	371	53.8	42.6	0.81	0.83	378	414
Portugal	135	297	9.7	15.3	0.91	1.32	146	313
Spain	211	321	33.4	30.1	1.15	1.19	245	352
Austria	307	394	80.3	65.7	1.22	1.18	389	461
Czechoslovakia	146	213	44.3	35.6	2.11	2.58	193	251
Finland	266	385	45.9	12.5	1.88	1.79	314	399
Hungary	103	195	61.8	16.1	2.20	2.34	167	213
Norway	311	380	37.2	38.9	3.14	5.48	352	424
Sweden	348	420	1.9	5.2	1.57	1.69	351	427
Switzerland	376	449	131.9	109.8	1.85	1.96	510	560
Yugoslavia	114	..	7.2	..	1.17	..	122	..
Japan	211	299	112.0	139.6	1.98	2.00	324	441
USA	538	578	25.4	16.5	2.37	2.50	565	597

Uses data from table 12 above, and consequently al the above footnotes apply.

39

Table 17 International comparisons: Road goods vehicles: 1981 and 1991

Thousands

	Rigid goods vehicles		Road tractors		Trailers & semi-trailers	
	1981	1991	1981	1991	1981	1991
Great Britain	1,676	2,210	95	100	..	..
Northern Ireland	37	45	2 [6]	3	..	..
United Kingdom	1,713	2,255	97	103	213	227
Belgium	223	..	18	..	56	..
Denmark [1]	238	..	10	..	141	..
France [2]	2,629	3,568 [6]	131	..	149	172
Germany	1,544	1,714	466	..	..	..
Former FRG	1,307	1,440	234	476	323 [11]	447 [11]
Former GDR	237	274	232	..	..	..
Greece	458	..	0.4	..	6.9	..
Irish Republic [3]	67	149	0.1	..	1.0	..
Italy	1,357	2,250 [6]	34	..	306	..
Luxembourg	9	13	3	7	..	..
Netherlands	316	542	23	38	74	..
Portugal	230	509 [6]	..	11 [6]	..	21 [6]
Spain	1,397	2,495	26	73	51	117
Total EC	11,725	..	..	..	..	..
Austria	190	259	340	389	177	312
Czechoslovakia	253	205	..	..	..	..
Finland [4]	152	262	3	..	25	362
Hungary	117	228	23 [8]	38 [8]	..	225 [6]
Norway	75	307	2	..	219	371
Sweden	183	310 [6]	4	4 [6]	270	450
Switzerland [5]	168	277	2 [9]	6 [9]	..	108
Yugoslavia	202	..	261 [10]	..	121	..
Japan	14,657	22,619	37	..	59	94
USA	34,451 [7]	45,619 [7]	1,237	1,353	2,597	3,608

1 Including imported second-hand vehicles.
2 Vehicles less than 10 years old.
3 Vehicles with a current licence only.
4 Tractors for semi-trailers included under rigid vehicles.
5 Semi-trailers and their tractors are included under rigid vehicles.
6 Extrapolated.
7 Includes light vans.
8 Tractors and trailers with a road registration number (including agricultural vehicles.)
9 Heavy industrial and agricultural tractors are included under tractors.
10 Including agricultral tractors provided with a road registration number.
11 Excluding 2 wheeled trailers with a standard body.

Table 18 Goods vehicle stock at end of year: 1982 - 1993

Thousands

Year	Rigids	Artics				All vehicles
		Not over 28 tonnes	28-37 tonnes	over 37 tonnes	All	
1982	347	12	76	- [1]	88	436
1983	348	11	68	10	89	436
1984	347	12	60	19	91	437
1985	341	12	52	26	90	432
1986 [2]	341	13	46	34	93	435
1987	346	14	43	41	98	444
1988	357	14	40	51	105	462
1989	368	14	36	60	110	478
1990 [2]	353	14	30	63	106	460
1991	330	13	26	61	100	430
1992	316	13	23	63	99	415
1993	313	12	21	64	98	410

1 Maximum Gross Vehicle Weight (GVW) was 32.5 tonnes until May 1983.

2 The analysis was delayed until the end of January the following year. Figures therefore include vehicles newly registered (about 3,000 in 1987 and 2,000 in 1991) or scrapped during the following January.

Trailers - analysis by axle type [1]

Thousands

National totals	1 axle	2 axle	3 axle	4 axle	5 axle	Total
First / Annual tests in 1992	13.1	132.2	75.6	0.1	-	221.0
First / Annual tests in 1993	12.0	128.5	83.7	0.1	-	224.3

1 This table is derived from Vehicle Inspectorate data on the number of trailers tested.
   Total stock at the end of 1991 was estimated to be between 230 and 240 thousand trailers.

Table 19 Goods vehicle stock: by gross weight and axle configuration: 1993

Thousands

Tractor	Trailer	Over Not over	3.5t 7.5t	7.5t 12t	12t 16t	16t 20t	20t 24t	24t 28t	28t 32t	32t 33t	33t 37t	37t 38t	38t	All weights
Rigid vehicles														
2 Axle			151.3	16.6	23.5	75.4	0.1	0.2	0.2	0.2	0.3	-	0.2	267.9
3 Axle			0.1	-	-	0.2	2.9	22.8	-	-	-	-	-	26.1
4 Axle			-	-	-	-	-	0.1	18.3	-	-	-	-	18.5
All			151.4	16.6	23.5	75.6	3.0	23.2	18.5	0.2	0.3	-	0.2	312.5
Articulated vehicles														
2 Axle	2 Axle		-	-	-	0.1	0.4	3.2	-	-	-	-	-	3.7
	3 Axle		-	-	-	-	-	0.2	0.1	0.6	1.2	33.8	-	35.9
	Any		0.2	-	0.1	1.5	0.7	5.8	1.0	17.1	0.1	2.1	-	28.7
All 2 Axle			0.2	-	0.1	1.7	1.1	9.1	1.1	17.7	1.3	35.9	-	68.3
3 Axle	2 Axle		-	-	-	-	-	-	-	0.2	0.1	-	-	0.4
	3 Axle		-	-	-	-	-	0.0	-	0.1	0.1	13.2	-	13.4
	Any		-	-	-	-	-	0.1	-	0.1	-	15.3	-	15.6
All 3 Axle			-	-	-	-	-	0.2	-	0.4	0.2	28.5	-	29.3
2 & 3 Axle	2 Axle		-	-	-	0.1	0.4	3.2	-	0.2	0.1	0.1	-	4.0
	3 Axle		-	-	-	-	-	0.2	0.1	0.6	1.3	47.0	-	49.2
	Any		0.2	-	0.1	1.5	0.8	5.9	1.0	17.2	0.2	17.4	-	44.3
All			0.2	-	0.1	1.7	1.1	9.3	1.1	18.1	1.5	64.4	-	97.5

41

Table 20 Goods vehicle stock: by taxation group and axle configuration: 1993

Thousands

Taxation class	Rigid vehicles				Articulated vehicles									
					2 axle tractor				3 axle tractor					
	2 axle	3 axle	4 axle	All	2 axle trailer	3 axle trailer	any trailer	All	2 axle trailer	3 axle trailer	any trailer	All	All	All
General goods														
1 HGV	237.3	23.8	17.7	278.8	3.6	35.5	27.2	66.3	0.3	13.3	15.3	28.9	95.2	374.0
2 Trailer HGV	5.0	1.0	-	5.9	-	-	-	-	-	-	-	-	-	6.0
Farmers goods														
3 HGV	10.7	0.6	0.3	11.5	0.1	0.4	0.6	1.0	-	0.1	0.1	0.2	1.3	12.8
4 Trailer HGV	0.2	0.1	-	0.3	-	-	-	-	-	-	-	-	-	0.3
Showmans goods														
5 HGV	0.6	-	-	0.7	-	-	-	0.1	-	-	-	-	0.1	0.7
6 Trailer HGV	0.0	-	-	-	-	-	-	-	-	-	-	-	-	-
Restricted														
7 HGV	3.7	0.2	0.1	4.0	-	-	0.2	0.2	-	-	-	-	0.2	4.2
8 HGV Farmers	0.2	-	-	0.2	-	-	-	-	-	-	-	-	-	0.2
9 HGV showmans	0.9	0.2	0.3	1.4	-	-	0.5	0.5	-	-	0.1	0.1	0.6	2.0
Others														
26 Goods (electric) [1]	0.9	-	-	0.9	-	-	-	-	-	-	-	-	-	0.9
60 Crown vehicles [1]	1.7	-	0.1	1.8	-	-	-	-	-	-	-	-	-	1.8
65-90 Exempt [1]	6.7	0.3	0.1	7.1	-	-	0.1	0.1	-	-	-	-	0.1	7.2
Total	267.9	26.1	18.5	312.5	3.7	35.9	28.7	68.3	0.4	13.4	15.6	29.3	97.5	410.1

1 Only vehicles in these taxation groups greater than 3500kg gross vehicle weight, and with goods vehicle body type.

Table 21 Goods vehicle stock: by gross vehicle weight and type of body: 1993

Thousands

Rigid vehicles

Body type	Over 3.5t Not over 7.5t	7.5t 12t	12t 16t	16t 20t	20t 24t	24t 28t	28t 32t	32t 33t	33t 37t	37t 38t	38t	All weights
Panel Van	6.2	0.1	0.1	0.2	-	0.2	0.1		0.3		-	7.2
Box body Van	54.4	6.5	7.8	21.6	0.4	1.1	0.1		-		-	92.0
Luton Van	3.0	0.3	0.6	0.3	-	-	-		-		-	4.3
Insulated Van	5.3	0.9	0.7	3.2	0.1	0.3	-		-		-	10.7
Van	4.3	0.4	0.7	0.6	-	0.1	-		-		-	6.1
Livestock Carrier	1.7	0.2	0.2	0.4	-	0.1	-		-		-	2.7
Float	3.8	-	-	0.1	-	-	-		-		0.1	4.1
Flat Lorry	11.5	2.0	2.4	9.2	0.5	2.2	1.2		-		-	28.9
Dropside Lorry	12.7	1.2	1.8	4.8	0.1	0.5	0.1		-		-	21.2
Tipper	22.1	1.4	3.6	8.3	0.1	8.0	11.7		-		-	55.3
Tanker	0.2	0.1	0.4	3.7	0.1	2.4	1.1		-		-	7.9
Refuse disposal	0.4	0.2	0.2	4.1	0.9	2.2	0.9		-		-	8.8
Goods	6.4	0.8	1.3	4.7	0.2	1.0	0.9		-		-	15.3
Skip loader	0.9	0.1	0.2	4.6	-	0.5	0.4		-		-	6.8
Others or not known	18.3	2.4	3.7	9.8	0.4	4.8	2.0	0.1			-	41.5
All body types	151.4	16.6	23.5	75.6	3.0	23.2	18.5		0.5		0.2	312.5

Articulated vehicles [1]

Body type	Over 3.5t Not over 7.5t	7.5t 12t	12t 16t	16t 20t	20t 24t	24t 28t	28t 32t	32t 33t	33t 37t	37t 38t	38t	All weights
Panel Van	-			-	-	-	-	-	-	-	-	-
Box body Van	0.1			0.3	0.2	1.7	0.2	3.0	0.4	4.7	-	10.6
Luton Van	-			-	-	-	-	-	-	-	-	-
Insulated Van	-			-	-	0.1	-	0.4	0.1	1.0	-	1.6
Van	-			-	-	0.1	-	0.1	-	0.3	-	0.4
Livestock Carrier	-			-	-	-	-	-	-	0.1	-	0.1
Float	-			-	-	-	-	-	-	-	-	0.1
Flat Lorry	-			0.2	0.1	0.6	0.1	1.8	0.1	7.3	-	10.2
Dropside Lorry	-			-	-	-	-	-	-	0.2	-	0.3
Tipper	0.1			-	-	0.1	-	0.1	-	2.2	-	2.5
Tanker	-			-	-	0.2	-	1.0	-	3.8	-	5.0
Refuse disposal	-			-	-	-	-	-	-	-	-	-
Goods	0.1			0.4	0.2	2.3	0.2	4.1	0.3	16.1	-	23.7
Skip loader	-			-	-	-	-	-	-	-	-	-
Others or not known	0.1			0.7	0.6	4.3	0.5	7.5	0.6	28.8	-	43.1
All body types	0.3			1.7	1.1	9.3	1.1	18.1	1.5	64.4	-	97.5

Rigid and articulated vehicles

Body type	Over 3.5t Not over 7.5t	7.5t 12t	12t 16t	16t 20t	20t 24t	24t 28t	28t 32t	32t 33t	33t 37t	37t 38t	38t	All weights
Panel Van	6.2	0.1	0.1	0.2	-	0.2	0.1	0.1	0.2	-	-	7.2
Box body Van	54.5	6.5	7.8	21.9	0.7	2.8	0.3	3.0	0.4	4.7	-	102.5
Luton Van	3.0	0.3	0.6	0.3	-	-	-	-	-	-	-	4.3
Insulated Van	5.3	0.9	0.7	3.3	0.1	0.4	-	0.4	0.1	1.0	-	12.3
Van	4.3	0.4	0.7	0.6	-	0.1	-	0.1	0.0	0.3	-	6.5
Livestock Carrier	1.7	0.2	0.2	0.4	-	0.1	-	-	-	0.1	-	2.8
Float	3.8	-	-	0.1	-	-	-	-	-	-	0.1	4.1
Flat Lorry	11.5	2.0	2.4	9.4	0.6	2.8	1.3	1.8	0.1	7.3	-	39.1
Dropside Lorry	12.7	1.2	1.8	4.8	0.1	0.5	0.1	-	-	0.2	-	21.4
Tipper	22.2	1.4	3.6	8.3	0.2	8.0	11.7	0.1	-	2.2	-	57.7
Tanker	0.2	0.1	0.4	3.7	0.1	2.5	1.1	1.0	-	3.8	-	12.9
Refuse disposal	0.4	0.2	0.2	4.1	0.9	2.2	0.9	-	-	0.0	-	8.8
Goods	6.4	0.8	1.3	5.1	0.4	3.3	1.1	4.1	0.3	16.1	-	39.0
Skip loader	0.9	0.1	0.2	4.6	-	0.5	0.4	-	-	-	-	6.8
Others or not known	18.4	2.4	3.7	10.5	0.9	9.1	2.5	7.6	0.6	28.8	-	84.5
All body types	151.6	16.6	23.6	77.3	4.1	32.5	19.6	18.3	1.8	64.5	0.2	410.1

1 Body type refers to that of the trailer, or most frequently used trailer.

Table 22 Goods vehicle stock: by GVW and year of 1st registration: 1993 [1]

Thousands

Year of first registration	Over 3.5t Not over 7.5t	7.5t 12t	12t 16t	16t 20t	20t 24t	24t 28t	28t 32t	32t 33t	33t 37t	37t 38t	38t ___	All weights
Rigid vehicles												
1983 and before	24.0	2.9	4.5	8.5	0.3	3.4	2.2		0.1		0.1	46.1
1984	8.0	0.9	1.7	4.5	0.1	1.5	0.9		-		-	17.6
1985	10.8	1.2	1.7	5.7	0.1	1.7	1.2		-		-	22.4
1986	11.7	1.5	2.0	6.4	0.2	2.0	1.6		-		-	25.4
1987	13.9	1.6	2.4	7.8	0.3	2.3	2.0		-		-	30.4
1988	17.8	1.6	2.6	9.9	0.3	2.9	2.9		-		-	38.1
1989	19.1	1.9	2.6	10.3	0.4	3.5	3.3		0.1		-	41.2
1990	15.1	1.6	2.1	7.7	0.4	2.2	1.6		-		-	30.8
1991	10.6	1.0	1.4	4.7	0.2	1.3	0.9		-		-	20.2
1992	10.3	1.1	1.3	4.7	0.3	1.1	0.8		0.1		-	19.7
1993	10.1	1.3	1.2	5.3	0.2	1.3	1.2		-		-	20.6
All years	151.4	16.6	23.5	75.6	3.0	23.2	18.5		0.5		0.2	312.5
Articulated vehicles (1)												
1983 and before		0.1		0.2	0.1	0.7	0.1	2.1	0.1	3.2	-	6.5
1984		-		0.1	-	0.3	-	0.9	-	2.9	-	4.3
1985		-		0.1	0.1	0.5	-	1.3	0.1	3.9	-	6.0
1986		-		0.2	0.1	0.7	0.1	1.5	-	4.5	-	7.1
1987		-		0.2	0.1	1.0	0.1	1.8	0.1	6.5	-	9.7
1988		-		0.2	0.1	1.0	0.1	2.5	0.1	9.1	-	13.3
1989		0.1		0.3	0.1	1.2	0.1	2.4	0.4	10.1	-	14.7
1990		-		0.1	0.1	1.0	0.1	1.6	0.1	6.4	-	9.5
1991		-		0.1	0.1	0.8	0.1	1.2	0.3	4.5	-	7.2
1992		-		0.1	0.1	0.9	0.1	1.3	0.2	5.7	-	8.4
1993		-		0.1	0.1	0.9	0.2	1.6	0.2	7.6	-	10.7
All years		0.3		1.7	1.1	9.3	1.1	18.1	1.5	64.4	-	97.5
Rigid and articulated vehicles												
1983 and before	24.1	2.9	4.5	8.7	0.4	4.1	2.3	2.2	0.1	3.3	0.1	52.6
1984	8.0	0.9	1.7	4.6	0.1	1.8	1.0	0.9	0.1	2.9	-	21.9
1985	10.8	1.2	1.7	5.8	0.2	2.3	1.2	1.3	0.1	3.9	-	28.5
1986	11.8	1.5	2.0	6.6	0.3	2.7	1.6	1.5	0.1	4.5	-	32.6
1987	14.0	1.6	2.4	7.9	0.4	3.3	2.1	1.8	0.1	6.5	-	40.2
1988	17.8	1.6	2.7	10.1	0.5	4.0	3.0	2.5	0.1	9.1	-	51.4
1989	19.2	1.9	2.6	10.6	0.5	4.7	3.4	2.5	0.4	10.1	-	55.9
1990	15.1	1.6	2.1	7.9	0.5	3.3	1.7	1.6	0.1	6.4	-	40.3
1991	10.6	1.0	1.4	4.9	0.3	2.1	1.0	1.2	0.3	4.5	-	27.4
1992	10.3	1.1	1.3	4.7	0.4	2.0	0.9	1.3	0.2	5.7	-	28.0
1993	10.1	1.3	1.2	5.4	0.3	2.2	1.4	1.6	0.2	7.6	-	31.3
All years	151.6	16.6	23.6	77.2	4.1	32.5	19.6	18.3	1.8	64.5	0.2	410.1

1 GVW: Gross vehicle weight.

Table 23 Goods vehicle stock: by year of 1st registration and type of body: 1993

Thousands

Body type	1983 & before	1984	1985	1986	1987	1988	1989	1990	1991	1992	1993	All years
Rigid vehicles												
Panel Van	0.5	0.2	0.4	0.5	0.8	0.9	1.1	1.0	0.7	0.6	0.5	7.2
Box body Van	6.9	3.8	5.4	6.2	8.6	12.3	13.4	10.4	7.7	8.3	9.0	92.0
Luton Van	1.3	0.3	0.4	0.3	0.4	0.5	0.4	0.3	0.2	0.1	0.1	4.3
Insulated Van	0.6	0.4	0.6	0.7	0.9	1.0	1.2	1.4	1.2	1.3	1.1	10.7
Van	1.9	0.5	0.5	0.5	0.7	0.5	0.4	0.4	0.2	0.2	0.2	6.1
Livestock Carrier	1.1	0.2	0.2	0.2	0.2	0.2	0.2	0.2	0.1	0.1	0.1	2.7
Float	2.5	0.2	0.2	0.2	0.2	0.3	0.2	0.1	0.1	0.1	-	4.1
Flat Lorry	7.8	2.5	2.8	2.6	2.7	3.0	3.0	1.9	0.9	0.8	0.8	28.9
Dropside Lorry	3.8	1.5	1.7	1.7	2.0	2.6	2.9	1.9	1.0	1.0	1.1	21.2
Tipper	9.3	3.6	4.2	4.6	5.1	7.0	8.0	4.9	3.0	2.3	3.1	55.3
Tanker	1.3	0.5	0.6	0.8	0.9	1.0	0.8	0.7	0.6	0.4	0.3	7.9
Refuse disposal	0.5	0.3	0.5	0.8	1.1	1.2	1.1	1.0	0.7	0.7	0.8	8.8
Goods	2.2	0.8	1.6	1.8	1.6	1.9	2.1	1.5	0.7	0.8	0.3	15.3
Skip loader	1.0	0.5	0.6	0.5	0.7	0.9	1.0	0.7	0.3	0.2	0.3	6.8
Others or not known	5.4	2.1	2.7	3.8	4.6	4.9	5.3	4.4	2.7	2.7	2.9	41.5
All body types	46.1	17.6	22.4	25.4	30.4	38.1	41.2	30.8	20.2	19.7	20.6	312.5
Articulated vehicles [1]												
Panel Van	-	-	-	-	-	-	-	-	-	-	-	-
Box body Van	0.4	0.3	0.5	0.5	0.8	1.5	1.7	1.0	1.1	1.3	1.6	10.6
Luton Van	-	-	-	-	-	-	-	-	-	-	-	-
Insulated Van	0.1	-	-	0.1	0.2	0.1	0.2	0.2	0.2	0.2	0.2	1.6
Van	0.1	-	-	-	0.1	-	-	-	-	-	-	0.4
Livestock Carrier	-	-	-	-	-	-	-	-	-	-	-	0.1
Float	-	-	-	-	-	-	-	-	-	-	-	0.1
Flat Lorry	2.0	0.9	1.0	1.0	1.1	1.3	1.0	0.7	0.4	0.4	0.4	10.2
Dropside Lorry	-	-	-	-	-	-	-	-	-	-	-	0.3
Tipper	0.2	0.1	0.2	0.2	0.2	0.4	0.4	0.3	0.1	0.1	0.2	2.5
Tanker	0.4	0.2	0.3	0.4	0.6	0.7	0.8	0.4	0.3	0.6	0.4	5.0
Refuse disposal	-	-	-	-	-	-	-	-	-	-	-	-
Goods	1.7	1.1	2.0	1.9	2.6	4.0	4.5	2.5	1.5	1.6	0.5	23.7
Skip loader	-	-	-	-	-	-	-	-	-	-	-	-
Others or not known	1.7	1.6	2.0	2.9	4.2	5.4	6.1	4.4	3.5	4.1	7.2	43.1
All body types	6.5	4.3	6.0	7.1	9.7	13.3	14.7	9.5	7.2	8.4	10.7	97.5
Rigid and articulated vehicles												
Panel Van	0.5	0.2	0.4	0.5	0.8	0.9	1.1	1.0	0.7	0.6	0.5	7.2
Box body Van	7.2	4.1	5.9	6.7	9.4	13.7	15.1	11.4	8.8	9.6	10.6	102.5
Luton Van	1.3	0.3	0.4	0.3	0.4	0.5	0.4	0.3	0.2	0.1	0.1	4.3
Insulated Van	0.7	0.4	0.6	0.8	1.1	1.1	1.4	1.6	1.4	1.5	1.4	12.3
Van	2.0	0.5	0.5	0.5	0.8	0.6	0.5	0.4	0.3	0.2	0.2	6.5
Livestock Carrier	1.1	0.2	0.2	0.2	0.2	0.2	0.2	0.2	0.1	0.1	0.1	2.8
Float	2.5	0.2	0.3	0.2	0.2	0.3	0.2	0.1	0.1	0.1	-	4.1
Flat Lorry	9.8	3.4	3.8	3.6	3.8	4.3	4.0	2.6	1.4	1.2	1.2	39.1
Dropside Lorry	3.9	1.5	1.7	1.7	2.0	2.6	2.9	1.9	1.0	1.0	1.2	21.4
Tipper	9.5	3.7	4.3	4.9	5.4	7.4	8.4	5.2	3.1	2.5	3.3	57.7
Tanker	1.7	0.8	0.9	1.3	1.4	1.6	1.6	1.1	0.9	1.0	0.7	12.9
Refuse disposal	0.5	0.3	0.5	0.8	1.1	1.2	1.1	1.0	0.7	0.7	0.8	8.8
Goods	3.9	2.0	3.5	3.7	4.1	5.8	6.6	4.0	2.2	2.4	0.8	39.0
Skip loader	1.0	0.5	0.6	0.5	0.7	1.0	1.0	0.7	0.3	0.2	0.3	6.8
Others or not known	7.1	3.8	4.7	6.7	8.8	10.2	11.4	8.9	6.2	6.8	10.1	84.6
All body types	52.6	21.9	28.5	32.6	40.2	51.4	55.9	40.3	27.4	28.0	31.3	410.1

1 Body type refers to that of the trailer, or most frequently used trailer.

Table 24 Goods vehicle stock: by county, region and axle configuration: 1993

Thousands

County/Region/Country	Rigid vehicles				Articulated vehicles									
					2 axle tractor				3 axle tractor					
	2 axle	3 axle	4 axle	All	2 axle trailer	3 axle trailer	any trailer	All	2 axle trailer	3 axle trailer	any trailer	All	All	All
Cleveland	1.57	0.22	0.10	1.90	0.02	0.59	0.26	0.87	-	0.07	0.21	0.28	1.15	3.05
Cumbria	2.23	0.35	0.21	2.79	0.04	0.77	0.24	1.05	-	0.30	0.37	0.67	1.71	4.50
Durham	2.08	0.29	0.30	2.67	0.10	0.56	0.18	0.84	-	0.12	0.24	0.37	1.20	3.88
Northumberland	0.94	0.14	0.16	1.23	0.01	0.23	0.07	0.31	-	0.07	0.08	0.15	0.46	1.70
Tyne and Wear	3.90	0.32	0.21	4.43	0.02	0.26	0.28	0.55	-	0.11	0.13	0.24	0.79	5.22
Northern	10.73	1.31	0.98	13.02	0.18	2.41	1.02	3.61	0.01	0.68	1.02	1.71	5.32	18.34
Humberside	2.98	0.40	0.25	3.63	0.04	1.19	0.31	1.54	-	0.59	0.64	1.24	2.78	6.40
North Yorkshire	4.87	0.73	0.43	6.02	0.05	1.10	0.33	1.48	0.01	0.33	0.35	0.68	2.16	8.19
South Yorkshire	6.00	0.52	0.49	7.00	0.11	0.75	0.74	1.60	0.01	0.26	0.58	0.84	2.44	9.44
West Yorkshire	15.97	0.85	0.50	17.32	0.11	1.79	1.42	3.32	0.08	0.55	0.63	1.25	4.58	21.90
Yorks and H'side	29.82	2.50	1.66	33.97	0.30	4.84	2.80	7.94	0.10	1.73	2.19	4.02	11.95	45.92
Derbyshire	4.25	0.46	0.53	5.24	0.02	0.52	0.49	1.02	-	0.19	0.29	0.49	1.51	6.75
Leicestershire	4.04	0.42	0.51	4.97	0.07	0.44	0.30	0.81	0.01	0.14	0.13	0.28	1.09	6.06
Lincolnshire	3.10	0.37	0.29	3.77	0.04	0.95	0.35	1.34	0.01	0.67	0.47	1.14	2.49	6.25
Northamptonshire	4.46	0.22	0.16	4.84	0.17	0.46	0.86	1.48	-	0.20	0.18	0.38	1.87	6.71
Nottinghamshire	5.68	0.45	0.28	6.41	0.05	0.54	0.53	1.12	0.01	0.15	0.28	0.43	1.56	7.97
East Midlands	21.53	1.93	1.76	25.22	0.35	2.91	2.52	5.78	0.02	1.35	1.35	2.72	8.51	33.73
Cambridgeshire	3.69	0.34	0.25	4.28	0.08	0.82	0.64	1.55	-	0.32	0.27	0.59	2.14	6.42
Norfolk	3.40	0.39	0.32	4.12	0.03	0.84	0.45	1.31	0.01	0.39	0.28	0.67	1.98	6.10
Suffolk	3.13	0.30	0.20	3.63	0.05	1.14	0.70	1.89	0.01	0.35	1.04	1.39	3.28	6.91
East Anglia	10.22	1.03	0.77	12.02	0.17	2.80	1.78	4.75	0.01	1.06	1.58	2.65	7.40	19.42
Bedfordshire	2.25	0.24	0.31	2.80	0.02	0.32	0.24	0.58	-	0.16	0.07	0.23	0.81	3.61
Berkshire	3.71	0.22	0.19	4.11	0.09	0.28	0.60	0.97	-	0.12	0.12	0.24	1.21	5.31
Buckinghamshire	3.36	0.37	0.28	4.01	0.04	0.70	0.52	1.26	-	0.10	0.14	0.24	1.50	5.50
East Sussex	2.31	0.12	0.08	2.51	0.01	0.12	0.06	0.19	-	0.08	0.02	0.11	0.30	2.80
Essex	5.95	0.59	0.69	7.22	0.07	1.01	0.69	1.76	0.02	0.51	0.51	1.04	2.80	10.03
Greater London	25.22	1.33	1.49	28.04	0.44	1.55	2.58	4.57	0.03	0.63	0.61	1.27	5.84	33.88
Hampshire	6.43	0.47	0.35	7.25	0.04	0.49	0.68	1.21	-	0.19	0.26	0.45	1.66	8.91
Hertfordshire	5.90	0.61	0.38	6.89	0.02	0.66	0.50	1.19	0.01	0.21	0.22	0.43	1.62	8.51
Isle of Wight	0.35	0.03	0.01	0.38	0.00	0.01	0.02	0.02	-	0.01	0.03	0.03	0.05	0.44
Kent	5.68	0.62	0.45	6.75	0.10	0.75	0.44	1.29	-	0.55	0.39	0.94	2.23	8.98
Oxfordshire	2.34	0.21	0.17	2.72	0.02	0.60	0.20	0.82	-	0.08	0.06	0.14	0.96	3.68
Surrey	4.91	0.78	0.28	5.96	0.01	0.57	0.28	0.86	-	0.05	0.10	0.15	1.01	6.97
West Sussex	2.06	0.15	0.14	2.34	0.03	0.12	0.16	0.31	-	0.05	0.03	0.08	0.39	2.73
South East	70.46	5.71	4.80	80.98	0.87	7.17	6.97	15.01	0.07	2.74	2.56	5.37	20.38	101.36
Avon	5.52	0.51	0.39	6.41	0.04	0.50	0.59	1.14	-	0.20	0.23	0.43	1.57	7.98
Cornwall	1.91	0.29	0.10	2.30	0.02	0.14	0.05	0.20	-	0.09	0.05	0.15	0.35	2.65
Devonshire	3.58	0.55	0.33	4.47	0.02	0.39	0.17	0.57	-	0.29	0.10	0.39	0.96	5.43
Dorset	2.20	0.23	0.09	2.51	0.01	0.20	0.09	0.30	-	0.12	0.03	0.15	0.46	2.97
Gloucestershire	2.33	0.39	0.18	2.90	0.04	0.32	0.22	0.58	-	0.15	0.11	0.26	0.84	3.73
Somerset	3.14	0.67	0.44	4.24	0.01	0.83	0.54	1.39	-	0.14	0.21	0.36	1.74	5.98
Wiltshire	4.18	0.31	0.20	4.69	0.12	0.32	0.65	1.09	-	0.14	0.18	0.32	1.40	6.09
South West	22.86	2.94	1.73	27.52	0.26	2.70	2.31	5.26	0.01	1.14	0.92	2.06	7.32	34.84

Table 24 (Cont'd) Goods vehicle stock: by county, region and axle configuration: 1993

Thousands

County	Rigid vehicles				Articulated vehicles									
					2 axle tractor				3 axle tractor					
	2 axle	3 axle	4 axle	All	2 axle trailer	3 axle trailer	any trailer	All	2 axle trailer	3 axle trailer	any trailer	All	All	All
Hereford & Worcs	3.37	0.43	0.17	3.97	0.05	0.36	0.57	0.97	0.01	0.19	0.24	0.43	1.40	5.38
Salop	3.37	0.50	0.23	4.10	0.04	0.46	0.37	0.87	-	0.26	0.34	0.60	1.47	5.57
Staffordshire	4.80	0.45	0.44	5.68	0.15	0.78	1.09	2.02	0.01	0.28	0.37	0.66	2.68	8.36
Warwickshire	2.24	0.17	0.14	2.55	0.07	0.29	0.55	0.90	-	0.14	0.16	0.30	1.20	3.75
West Midlands	19.27	2.04	1.19	22.49	0.18	1.50	2.09	3.76	0.02	0.54	0.47	1.02	4.79	27.28
West Midlands	33.05	3.58	2.16	38.80	0.48	3.38	4.66	8.53	0.04	1.41	1.58	3.02	11.54	50.34
Cheshire	5.06	0.56	0.36	5.97	0.13	0.89	0.59	1.61	0.02	0.33	0.45	0.79	2.40	8.37
Gtr Manchester	15.76	0.97	0.84	17.57	0.29	1.42	1.98	3.70	0.04	0.40	0.89	1.33	5.02	22.59
Lancashre	7.57	0.57	0.50	8.65	0.14	0.98	0.63	1.74	0.01	0.36	0.67	1.04	2.79	11.44
Merseyside	4.03	0.34	0.41	4.78	0.09	0.75	0.54	1.39	-	0.21	0.33	0.55	1.93	6.72
North Western	32.42	2.45	2.11	36.98	0.65	4.04	3.74	8.43	0.07	1.29	2.35	3.71	12.14	49.12
England	231.09	21.45	15.96	268.50	3.27	30.24	25.81	59.32	0.32	11.39	13.54	25.26	84.57	353.07
Borders	0.55	0.10	0.01	0.66	-	0.09	0.04	0.13	-	0.03	0.03	0.06	0.19	0.84
Central Scotland	1.27	0.20	0.14	1.61	0.01	0.29	0.16	0.46	-	0.10	0.14	0.24	0.70	2.31
Dumfries & Galloway	1.07	0.15	0.08	1.30	0.03	0.19	0.06	0.28	-	0.08	0.13	0.21	0.49	1.79
Fife	0.92	0.18	0.12	1.22	0.01	0.19	0.06	0.26	-	0.03	0.07	0.11	0.36	1.59
Grampain	2.45	0.45	0.26	3.16	0.01	0.91	0.23	1.15	-	0.41	0.16	0.57	1.72	4.88
Highland	0.97	0.17	0.08	1.21	-	0.15	0.02	0.18	-	0.06	0.06	0.12	0.30	1.51
Lothian	2.83	0.30	0.17	3.30	0.02	0.37	0.24	0.63	-	0.09	0.10	0.19	0.82	4.13
Orkney	0.13	0.05	0.01	0.18	-	-	0.01	0.02	-	-	-	-	0.02	0.20
Shetland	0.17	0.04	0.01	0.22	-	-	0.02	0.02	-	0.00	0.01	0.01	0.03	0.25
Strathclyde	8.41	1.02	0.57	9.99	0.08	1.12	0.64	1.83	-	0.35	0.58	0.94	2.77	12.76
Tayside	1.63	0.28	0.08	2.00	0.01	0.32	0.10	0.42	-	0.13	0.08	0.21	0.63	2.63
Western Isles	0.18	0.05	0.01	0.24	-	0.01	0.01	0.02	-	0.02	0.00	0.02	0.05	0.29
Scotland	20.59	2.99	1.53	25.10	0.17	3.64	1.58	5.40	0.02	1.31	1.36	2.69	8.08	33.19
Clwyd	1.64	0.23	0.22	2.09	0.03	0.24	0.32	0.60	-	0.10	0.10	0.20	0.80	2.88
Dyfed	1.94	0.28	0.12	2.34	0.02	0.29	0.09	0.39	-	0.07	0.11	0.19	0.58	2.93
Gwent	1.89	0.18	0.10	2.16	0.07	0.41	0.17	0.65	-	0.13	0.07	0.21	0.85	3.01
Gwynedd	1.11	0.10	0.09	1.31	0.01	0.04	0.03	0.08	-	0.01	0.04	0.04	0.12	1.43
Mid Glamorgan	1.69	0.25	0.15	2.09	0.05	0.24	0.17	0.46	-	0.05	0.04	0.10	0.56	2.64
Powys	1.04	0.18	0.06	1.28	0.01	0.09	0.05	0.15	-	0.05	0.03	0.07	0.23	1.51
South Glamorgan	1.68	0.10	0.05	1.83	0.01	0.16	0.10	0.27	-	0.05	0.04	0.09	0.36	2.19
West Glamorgan	1.07	0.09	0.06	1.22	0.01	0.11	0.07	0.18	-	0.04	0.08	0.12	0.30	1.52
Wales	12.06	1.41	0.84	14.31	0.22	1.58	0.98	2.78	0.01	0.51	0.50	1.02	3.79	18.11
County unknown	0.28	0.04	0.01	0.33	-	0.07	0.02	0.09	-	0.03	0.02	0.05	0.13	0.46
No current keeper vehicle under disposal	3.86	0.25	0.19	4.30	0.04	0.34	0.31	0.68	-	0.13	0.14	0.28	0.95	5.26
Great Britain	267.87	26.14	18.54	312.54	3.69	35.87	28.70	68.25	0.35	13.36	15.57	29.28	97.53	410.08

Table 25 Goods vehicle stock at end of year: 1983-1993: by year of 1st registration

Thousands

Rigid vehicles

Year of 1st registration	1983	1984	1985	1986	1987	1988	1989	1990	1991	1992	1993
Pre 1976	73.9	55.5	55.1	54.0	61.6	71.4	73.8	62.9	57.6	57.9	63.7
1976	23.7	19.2									
1977	29.4	25.0	19.9								
1978	38.9	34.9	29.5	23.6							
1979	48.7	45.6	41.0	35.4	30.3						
1980	39.7	38.3	35.8	32.3	28.7	24.1					
1981	29.7	29.0	28.0	26.2	24.2	21.4	18.4				
1982	29.9	29.3	28.7	27.7	26.3	24.4	21.7	17.5			
1983	33.5	33.3	32.8	32.1	31.3	29.7	27.4	23.4	19.4		
1984		36.4	35.1	34.6	34.1	33.1	30.9	27.4	23.5	20.5	
1985			35.6	36.4	36.1	35.2	33.9	31.2	28.1	25.1	22.4
1986				38.8	36.4	35.8	34.7	33.2	30.5	28.0	25.4
1987					37.6	37.8	37.3	35.9	34.2	32.2	30.4
1988						44.0	44.5	43.1	41.5	39.8	38.1
1989							45.1	44.8	43.4	42.2	41.2
1990								33.8	31.6	31.2	30.8
1991									20.0	20.2	20.2
1992										19.1	19.7
1993											20.6
All years	347.6	346.5	341.3	341.1	346.5	357.0	367.6	353.3	329.9	316.2	312.5

Articulated vehicles

Year of 1st registration	1983	1984	1985	1986	1987	1988	1989	1990	1991	1992	1993
Pre 1976	7.7	4.7	5.0	5.9	8.7	11.5	11.5	9.4	8.9	9.5	10.8
1976	4.9	3.5									
1977	8.3	6.3	4.3								
1978	12.3	10.3	7.9	5.8							
1979	15.3	13.9	11.6	9.3	7.7						
1980	10.8	10.4	9.1	7.8	6.6	5.2					
1981	8.7	8.4	7.8	7.0	6.2	5.2	3.9				
1982	9.9	9.7	9.4	9.0	8.3	7.4	6.1	4.4			
1983	10.8	10.9	10.6	10.3	9.9	9.1	7.8	6.0	4.4		
1984		12.5	11.9	11.7	11.5	11.0	10.1	8.4	6.7	5.6	
1985			12.8	12.8	12.7	12.3	11.7	10.5	8.7	7.5	6.0
1986				13.7	12.6	12.4	11.8	11.0	9.7	8.6	7.1
1987					13.9	14.0	13.6	12.8	11.9	11.0	9.7
1988						16.7	16.7	16.2	15.4	14.6	13.3
1989							17.2	16.8	16.3	15.9	14.7
1990								11.1	10.2	10.1	9.5
1991									7.4	7.4	7.2
1992										8.5	8.4
1993											10.7
All years	88.6	90.7	90.4	93.5	97.9	104.6	110.4	106.5	99.7	98.7	97.5

Rigid and articulated vehicles

Year of 1st registration	1983	1984	1985	1986	1987	1988	1989	1990	1991	1992	1993
Pre 1976	81.6	60.2	60.1	59.9	70.3	82.9	88.1	72.3	66.4	67.4	74.5
1976	28.7	22.7									
1977	37.6	31.3	24.2								
1978	51.3	45.2	37.4	29.3							
1979	64.0	59.5	52.6	44.8	37.9						
1980	50.7	48.7	44.9	40.1	35.2	29.3					
1981	38.3	37.4	35.8	33.2	30.4	26.6	22.3				
1982	39.7	39.0	38.0	36.7	34.6	31.8	27.7	21.9			
1983	44.3	44.1	43.4	42.4	41.2	38.8	35.2	29.4	23.9		
1984		48.9	47.0	46.4	45.5	44.0	41.0	35.8	30.3	26.0	
1985			48.4	49.2	48.7	47.5	45.5	41.7	36.8	32.6	28.5
1986				52.5	48.9	48.2	46.5	44.2	40.2	36.6	32.6
1987					51.4	51.7	50.9	48.7	46.1	43.2	40.2
1988						60.7	61.2	59.3	56.9	54.4	51.4
1989							62.3	61.6	59.8	58.1	55.9
1990								44.8	41.8	41.3	40.3
1991									27.4	27.6	27.4
1992										27.6	28.0
1993											31.3
All years	436.3	437.1	431.7	434.6	444.4	461.6	478.0	459.7	429.6	414.9	410.1

Table 26 Goods vehicle stock at end of year: 1984-1993: by gross vehicle weight

Thousands

Over	Not over	1984	1985	1986	1987	1988	1989	1990	1991	1992	1993
Rigid vehicles											
3.5t	7.5t	145.7	146.9	150.8	155.0	161.9	169.5	166.2	157.8	152.0	151.4
7.5t	12t	32.7	29.3	26.4	24.9	23.3	22.0	20.1	18.5	17.2	16.6
12t	16t	46.6	42.8	39.2	36.7	34.5	32.2	29.2	26.0	24.3	23.5
16t	20t	77.4	78.5	80.1	82.8	86.7	89.9	87.1	80.9	77.9	75.6
20t	24t	1.1	0.9	1.0	1.4	1.8	2.1	2.4	2.5	2.7	3.0
24t	28t	26.1	25.6	25.6	26.2	27.2	28.3	26.6	24.5	23.3	23.2
28t	32t	16.8	17.2	17.9	19.4	21.6	23.5	21.5	19.5	18.6	18.5
32t		0.1	0.1	0.1	0.1	0.1	0.2	0.2	0.2	0.2	0.6
All weights		346.5	341.3	341.1	346.5	357.0	367.6	353.3	329.9	316.2	312.5
Articulated vehicles											
3.5t	16t	0.6	0.6	0.6	0.5	0.5	0.5	0.5	0.4	0.3	0.3
16t	20t	4.9	4.5	4.1	3.7	3.1	2.8	2.4	2.1	1.9	1.7
20t	24t	0.9	1.0	1.1	1.1	1.1	1.0	1.1	1.0	1.1	1.1
24t	28t	5.4	6.3	7.3	8.4	9.1	9.7	9.7	9.2	9.3	9.3
28t	32t	2.5	1.8	1.5	1.3	1.1	1.1	0.9	0.9	1.0	1.1
32t	33t	55.7	48.7	43.7	40.5	37.3	33.5	28.1	23.2	19.9	18.1
33t	37t	1.2	1.2	1.3	1.3	1.2	1.5	1.4	1.5	1.7	1.5
37t	38t	19.4	26.3	33.9	41.2	51.1	60.3	62.5	61.3	63.5	64.4
38t		-	-	-	-	-	-	-	-	-	-
All weights		90.7	90.4	93.5	97.9	104.6	110.4	106.5	99.7	98.7	97.5
Rigid and articulated vehicles											
3.5t	7.5t	146.0	147.2	151.0	155.3	162.1	169.8	166.4	158.1	152.2	151.6
7.5t	12t	33.0	29.5	26.6	25.1	23.4	22.1	20.2	18.5	17.2	16.6
12t	16t	46.7	42.9	39.3	36.8	34.6	32.4	29.3	26.1	24.4	23.6
16t	20t	82.3	82.9	84.2	86.4	89.8	92.6	89.5	83.0	79.8	77.2
20t	24t	2.0	2.0	2.1	2.5	2.8	3.1	3.4	3.5	3.8	4.1
24t	28t	31.5	31.9	32.9	34.5	36.3	38.1	36.3	33.7	32.7	32.5
28t	32t	19.2	19.0	19.4	20.7	22.7	24.6	22.4	20.4	19.5	19.6
32t	38t	76.4	76.2	79.0	83.1	89.7	95.5	92.2	86.2	85.3	84.6
38t		0.1	0.1	-	-	-	-	-	-	-	0.2
All weights		437.1	431.7	434.6	444.4	461.6	478.0	459.7	429.6	414.9	410.1

Table 27 Goods vehicles stock at end of year: 1988-1993: by gross vehicle weight, axle configuration

Thousands

Axles	Year	Over / Not over	3.5 / 7.5	7.5 / 12	12 / 16	16 / 20	20 / 24	24 / 28	28 / 32	32 / 33	33 / 37	37 / 38	38	All weights
Rigid vehicles														
2 Axle	1988		165.2	23.4	36.3	85.6	-	-	-	-	-	-	-	310.5
	1989		169.9	21.6	33.1	87.1	-	-	-	-	-	-	-	311.7
	1990		167.5	20.2	30.1	85.1	-	-	-	-	-	-	-	302.9
	1991		160.3	18.5	26.7	79.1	0.1	0.3	0.2	-	-	-	-	285.2
	1992		155.3	17.2	25.0	76.9	0.1	0.3	0.2	-	-	-	-	275.0
	1993		151.3	16.6	23.5	75.4	0.1	0.2	0.2	0.2	0.3	-	0.2	268.0
3 Axles	1988		0.1	-	0.2	0.3	1.8	26.5	-	-	-	-	-	28.9
	1989		0.1	-	0.1	0.3	2.1	26.8	-	-	-	-	-	29.4
	1990		0.1	-	0.1	0.3	2.3	25.6	-	-	-	-	-	28.4
	1991		0.1	-	0.1	0.3	2.4	23.5	-	-	-	-	-	26.4
	1992		0.1	-	-	0.2	2.7	22.9	-	-	-	-	-	26.0
	1993		0.1	-	-	0.2	2.9	22.8	-	-	-	-	-	26.1
4 Axles	1988		-	-	-	-	-	0.5	21.3	-	-	-	-	21.8
	1989		-	-	-	-	-	0.3	22.3	-	-	-	-	22.6
	1990		-	-	-	-	-	0.2	20.6	-	-	-	-	20.8
	1991		-	-	-	-	-	0.2	18.6	-	-	-	-	18.8
	1992		-	-	-	-	-	0.2	18.3	-	-	-	-	18.5
	1993		-	-	-	-	-	0.1	18.3	-	-	-	-	18.5
All	1988		165.3	23.5	36.5	85.8	2.2	27.5	21.6	-	-	-	-	362.4
	1989		170.0	21.6	33.3	87.4	2.4	27.7	22.6	-	-	-	-	365.0
	1990		167.6	20.2	30.2	85.4	2.5	26.2	20.9	-	-	-	-	353.0
	1991		160.4	18.6	26.8	79.3	2.6	24.0	18.8	-	-	-	-	330.5
	1992		155.4	17.3	25.0	77.1	2.8	23.4	18.5	-	-	-	-	319.5
	1993		151.4	16.6	23.5	75.6	3	23.2	18.5	0.2	0.3	-	0.2	312.5
Articulated vehicles														
2 Axle tractive units	1988			0.5		3.0	1.0	8.9	1.1	35.4	1.0	31.2	-	82.0
	1989			0.5		2.6	0.9	9.2	0.9	30.8	1.2	34.6	-	80.8
	1990			0.5		2.3	1.0	9.0	0.8	26.1	1.2	34.8	-	75.7
	1991			0.4		2.0	1.0	8.8	0.7	21.3	1.3	33.5	-	69.0
	1992			0.3		1.8	1.0	8.8	0.9	18.4	1.5	34.8	-	67.5
	1993			0.3		1.7	1.1	9.1	1.1	17.7	1.3	35.9	-	68.3
3 Axles tractive units	1988			-		-	-	-	-	0.3	0.2	19.1	-	19.6
	1989			-		-	-	0.1	-	0.3	0.1	23.4	-	23.9
	1990			-		-	-	0.1	-	0.3	0.2	25.3	-	25.8
	1991			-		-	-	0.1	-	0.3	0.2	25.1	-	25.7
	1992			-		-	-	0.2	-	0.3	0.2	26.7	-	27.3
	1993			-		-	-	0.2	-	0.4	0.2	28.5	-	29.3
All	1988			0.5		3.0	1.0	9.0	1.0	35.6	1.2	50.3	-	101.7
	1989			0.5		2.6	0.9	9.3	0.9	31.0	1.4	57.9	-	104.7
	1990			0.5		2.3	1.0	9.1	0.8	26.4	1.3	60.1	-	101.5
	1991			0.4		2.0	1.0	8.9	0.7	21.6	1.5	58.6	-	94.7
	1992			0.3		1.9	1.0	8.9	0.9	18.6	1.6	61.5	-	94.8
	1993			0.3		1.7	1.1	9.3	1.1	18.1	1.5	64.4	-	97.5

Printed in the United Kingdom for HMSO
Dd 300073 C3.5 10/94 17434